NAMES AND FACES MADE EASY

A FUN AND EASY WAY to Remember People

JERRY LUCAS – DR. MEMORY™

Learning That Lasts™

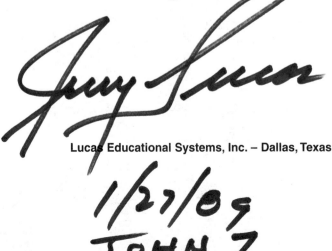

Lucas Educational Systems, Inc. – Dallas, Texas

1/27/09
JOHN 7

Published by:

LUCAS EDUCATIONAL SYSTEMS, INC.
Post Office Box 794747
Dallas, Texas 75248 U.S.A.

Library of Congress Card Number: 00-104325
ISBN: 1-930853-01-7

Lucas, Jerry
Names & Faces Made Easy
First Edition

Dedication

To all people everywhere who have struggled with trying to remember names.

Acknowledgements

I wish to express my gratitude to all of the people over the years who have helped me. Bill Murray, who has been my right arm for twenty years; Rolland Dingman, Mike Webster, Tony Price and Jon McIntosh who have brought the pictures in my mind to life in so many projects; Robert Wiley, who has assisted me in so many ways; and my wife, Cheri, who has always believed with me.

Contents

About the Author

As a boy with a very active mind, NBA legend Jerry Lucas challenged himself by inventing mental games to test his memory. At an early age, Jerry realized that being a successful student in school took knowing not only HOW to learn but also HOW TO RETAIN that learned information. He became determined to develop ways to make the learning process EASY, FUN and LONG-LASTING.

Like a farmer who plants small seeds in the soil and carefully tends them so that they grow, Jerry has devoted his life to cultivating ideas and methods for fun and easy memory-retention methods. The resulting methods are now known as **The Lucas Learning System**™ and have earned him the title of **Doctor Memory**™.

Jerry graduated Phi Beta Kappa from Ohio State University. Not only a scholastic achiever, he excelled as an athlete as well. Jerry became the only basketball player in collegiate history to lead the nation in field goal percentage and rebounding for three years, thus becoming the only three-time recipient of the Big Ten player-of-the-year award. This achievement still has not been duplicated or surpassed. Chosen seven times as an All-Pro during his professional basketball career, Jerry was named one of the 50 most outstanding NBA players of all time. Being inducted into the NBA Hall of Fame in 1979 was perhaps his crowning achievement as an athlete.

Recently, Jerry was chosen as one of the five most outstanding college basketball players of the twentieth century by *Sports Illustrated* in its article entitled "Team of the Ages," which appeared in the November, 1999 College Basketball preview issue.

Although Mr. Lucas initially achieved fame and success by his impressive basketball accomplishments, he continues to score off the court as well. Through the years, Jerry has taught his memory-retention system to millions of people either in seminars or through sales of his books. Not only did he co-author the *New York Times* best-seller *The Memory Book*, he also has entertained countless television viewers with guest appearances on TV talk shows during which he dazzled large numbers of studio audience members by demonstrating his ability to meet and remember all of their names.

In total, Jerry Lucas has authored more than sixty books in the field of memory training and learning systems. **Doctor Memory**™ is now widely known and respected as an expert in developing the many methods that encompass his concept known as **Learning That Lasts**™ .

Foreword
Bill Bradley

When I think of Jerry Lucas, I think of not only his earlier bestseller in collaboration with Harry Lorayne called The Memory Book, but I also recall my own experience with Jerry and his incredible memory and learning capabilities.

In particular, I remember one night after a Knick's game in New York when my wife, Ernestine, and I were at a party and Bobby Fisher, the great chess player was also in attendance. Jerry Lucas told Bobby Fisher that he had memorized the phone numbers in the first column of the first seventy pages of the Manhattan telephone directory. Fisher responded in disbelief, claiming that it was impossible — it just couldn't be done. Lucas replied, "Ok, go to the first seventy pages and look at the first column on each page — pick a number and tell me how many names down from the top of the selected page it is, and I'll tell you the telephone number." Fisher expressing his serious doubts picked up the telephone directory, selected page 49 and scrolled down with his index finger to the 52nd name. Lucas replied 581-3211 – which was the exact number. That is when I first realized that Jerry Lucas had an extraordinary memory.

"I bet you don't remember my name." I've heard that challenge from constituents and fans for 30 years. You don't have to be a politician to understand how important it is to remember someone's name. Just ask any salesperson or doctor or entrepreneur. It's just good common sense.

Jerry's book, *Names & Faces Made Easy*, is full of insightful techniques to help individuals have a fun and easy way to remember names. The more you can remember names and faces, the more comfortable you'll be meeting people. His proven techniques have already been used by millions of people.

CHAPTER 1

The Present Day
Educational Dilemma

When a child enters school he or she is normally very excited and full of anticipation for this new **learning** experience in his or her life. But far too quickly almost every student begins to make comments like, "I don't like this," or "This is no fun." Unfortunately, a young mind full of unlimited imagination and potential begins to turn off and tune out. Worst of all, children are not generally taught **How to Learn**, even though that is the proposed reason for going to school in the first place. Since a student is not taught **How to Learn**, he or she has to rely on boring repetition while trying to remember the necessary information to pass tests and become educated. It is not the fault of the many wonderful and dedicated teachers. They were never taught **How to Learn** either, so they can't teach what they in turn don't know.

The child, the child's parents and the child's teachers are not generally aware that the basic method of learning employed prior to entering school is altered forever after entering school. The method of learning in the home prior to school and the method of learning after entering school are diametrically opposed to one another. The **"learning battle"** doesn't really begin until a child enters school, and tragically, it doesn't have to be a battle at all. What began with such great expectations far too soon turns into a dull, lifeless routine. Can this process be changed? Yes! **Learning really can be fun**. Learning and laughing at the same time or laughing during the process of learning are not unnatural. It will happen more and more in schools, homes, churches and places of business when The Lucas Learning System™ is applied.

There are only three steps in the educational process. They are:

1) Getting information
2) Learning the information
3) Using the information that has been learned

Unfortunately there is a great chasm or abyss in our present day educational system between steps 1 and 3. **Getting information** is no problem. It is given to us in textbooks and other printed material. **Learning the information**, since we are not taught how to learn, becomes the boring, repetitive, non-productive process that we have become all too familiar with. The rote process may enable us to remember the information long enough to pass a test, but it leaves our minds in short order, and we can't really **use the**

information, because it hasn't really been learned. **You can't use what you lose**. Unfortunately, students try to learn and relearn the same information, such as the rules of capitalization, year after year. Not only do they forget most of it shortly after taking a test, but they graduate from high school, if indeed they do graduate, having forgotten or lost most of it. Students keep falling back into the chasm or abyss of unlearned information as shown in the drawing below. Eventually they get tired of crawling out of this hole time and time again.

What they hoped to have learned was only crammed into their minds for a very short period of time. It didn't become knowl-

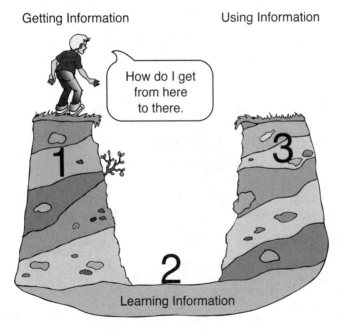

Getting Information

Using Information

How do I get from here to there.

1

3

2

Learning Information

edge. Students fall back into the chasm or abyss and have to climb back out time and time again. After a period of time and repeated failures, many of them simply give up and mentally drop out, which causes an alarming number to literally and physically drop out of school. When that happens the results are often disastrous.

Our prisons and welfare rolls are testaments to our failure in this area. If they don't give up but keep fighting this uphill battle, they take their learning frustrations into their adult lives and careers. Business and industry then spends billions of dollars trying to accomplish what wasn't accomplished in school. But, unfortunately, the same repetitive processes continue to be used in business and industry, and the results are less than satisfactory. That is why you have a problem remembering such things as names and faces.

Everyone is attracted to what is enjoyable and rewarding in his or her life. It is my contention, that we can and will change one of the most difficult and discouraging dilemmas facing America today. I believe you will agree with this statement after reading and applying the principles and learning systems taught in this book. We can make learning fun and rewarding. We can change young lives and give them hope instead of despair. We can teach students how to face, attack and solve learning problems effectively and efficiently. Even though this book is not about our educational needs but about remembering names and faces, you will see a few examples and get some incite into why I believe this is true.

For example, if you have a mechanical problem with your automobile, you need to take it to a qualified mechanic who possesses the knowledge and has the proper tools with which to find and repair problems in your car. One problem may require a simple tool like a screwdriver or a wrench. Other problems may require much more sophisticated and perhaps even electronic tools. The correct tool or tools are selected from his toolbox to solve or repair each problem. You will feel much more at ease if you can find a **master mechanic**, because he certainly will not only have the tools for the job, but he will possess extraordinary skill with which to use them.

In education and in our social and business lives there are a variety of learning problems that need to be solved or fixed, if you will, like mechanical problems in a car. They include learning how to read and write, how to spell, grammar and punctuation rules, English and foreign vocabulary, definitions, formulas, the periodic table in chemistry, lists, numbers, muscle location, graphs, speeches, magazines or manuals, **names and faces**, dates and calendars and much more. Of course, the list goes on and on. Which learning tool did you use to learn definitions? Which learning tool did you use to learn formulas? Which learning tool did you use to learn vocabulary? For the subject matter of this book, which learning tool did you use to remember names and faces? The **tool** you used for each and every learning problem in the past is **a Stone Age tool** at best. It is the **Stone Age axe of repetition**. If we were **auto mechanics** we would be out of business in a hurry if we had only Stone Age tools, because we wouldn't possess the up-to-date tools to correct problems and be able to compete with more qualified mechanics, especially **Master Mechanics**. We approach every learning problem, even after years of school, by using repetition. This boring, rote-type process dulls the senses and defeats the user. Unfortunately, your basic ability to learn and your knowledge of how to learn haven't changed much since you entered school. Yes, you have slugged it out with repetition over the years, but you are still using the Stone Age axe of repetition to try to learn. You have a very limited **mental toolbox**. Fortunately, there are **legitimate tools of learning** to select for various learning problems much like an auto mechanic selects the proper tool from his toolbox for his various needs. These **learning tools** enable the user to analyze, attack and solve any learning problem effectively, efficiently and with confidence. Most importantly, the user will experience rewarding, satisfying results as he or she selects the appropriate tool from a complete array of tools in his or her **mental toolbox**. My goal with this book is to make you a **Master Mind Mechanic** who knows how to easily remember names and faces, not with the **Stone Age axe of repetition** but with **sophisticated**, **modern**, **high-tech learning tools**. It is time for a change, a much needed, refreshing and life-changing change.

In reality, we are still in the Stone Age as far as learning is concerned. So many incredible advances have occurred in other areas, but we still attempt to learn with repetition. Yes, we do have better repetition equipment like computers, but they still haven't changed the basic problem. It is time to **get out of the Stone Age** as far as learning is concerned and move into **high tech, up-to-date learning** methods available with **The Lucas Learning System**™.

This book is not intended to be a slam on the teachers of America. I admire America's teachers. They are interested in the youth of America, wield considerable influence on their lives, and most of them are highly dedicated, underpaid in my opinion, and do the best job possible under the circumstances. Unfortunately, they cannot teach what they have not been taught. Teachers, like the rest of us, were not taught learning systems when they were in school. They had to use the Stone Age axe of repetition to pass tests like everyone else. A teacher cannot teach what he or she has not been taught. Teachers are more or less reduced to the roles of drill sergeants making comments like, "Just go over it" or "Say it repeatedly until you know it." Such attempted learning is no fun and becomes stressful for the teacher, the student and the parent who tries to help. This process develops a lack of confidence, a lack of self-esteem and causes people to grow into adulthood making statements like, "I can't seem to remember anything," or "I have a terrible memory." People don't have bad memories, just untrained ones.

This book will teach you names and faces applications that go way beyond what was taught in *The Memory Book*. I have sophisticated and improved my ability to remember names and faces by developing many new applications since *The Memory Book* was published in 1973.

CHAPTER 2

How It All Began for Me

As a boy I had a very active mind like most children, but the release of my mental energies began to be a little bit different from most people. I began to invent mental games to keep me occupied when I was bored, especially during long automobile trips. On one particular long vacation trip with nothing to do, I saw a word on a billboard and got an idea. I wondered what the word would look like if I mentally rearranged the letters in the word and put them in alphabetical order. So with my little grade school mind, I began to mentally rearrange the letters in alphabetical order. I did it, saw another word on a billboard and rearranged the letters alphabetically in that word as well. I continued to do it with other words I saw the rest of that trip. Some words were too long and complicated for me to even attempt at first, but I got hooked after that day and continued to do it every day of my life without anyone knowing it. Neither my parents nor my brother knew I was doing it. It was something to do to relieve boredom.

That mental game lead to many others in time. Suffice it to say that my mind was always active with some mental game or activity. As a matter of fact, I got so good that I could spell words alphabetically faster than others could regularly. I could spell them so fast that the letters blurred together and others couldn't decipher the letters I was calling out. I had to deliberately slow down so I could be understood. I will explain later how others began to discover that I spelled alphabetically.

I say all of this to let you understand that my mind was very active and looking for activity to keep it occupied. I began to realize that memory and learning was becoming more and more important to me as a student in grade school. I also began to realize that I was not being taught "How to Learn." My teachers weren't saying things like, "Here is what you have to learn for your next test and here is how to learn it." They were saying things like, "Here is what you have to learn for your next test. The test will be on Friday." No further help was forthcoming except maybe some repetitive drills in class. Learning the material was being left up to me. I was on my own. What did that mean? Repetition - repetition - repetition. I didn't like it and neither did my classmates, but what could we possibly do? I didn't know, but I sure didn't like what I had to do to pass my tests. I was doing well on tests because I was diligent, but eventually I said to myself, "There has to be an easier, more fun and long-lasting way of learning than repetition," and the greatest adventure of my life began. I was determined to think of ways to make the learning process easy, fun and long-lasting. That meant experimentation and lots of trial and error. Now my active mind had a real adventure to explore, a real challenge. That simple beginning, that small seed has grown into **The Lucas Learning System**™.

At first, since I was so good at alphabetical spelling, I began to take the first letter of each word in lists I needed to remember and place them in alphabetical order. I remembered the alphabetical list, and it was a memory aid that helped lead me to the actual list, because the alphabetized letters triggered the information in the list. I wouldn't know for years that I was using a very basic **anagram** device. An **anagram** learning device is a word or phrase developed by rearranging the beginning letters of a word, phrase or list. As a young boy I began to use that idea without realizing what it was. Since this idea was limited in its application, I began to experiment with other ideas, be involved in trial and error and eventually began to research memory training. Through the years, **The Lucas Learning System**™ began to take form and become reality.

Several people have taught general applications using memory aids of one kind or another that have been helpful, but I believe my contribution to learning has been the development of unique, in-depth systems and applications that not only solve learning problems but also specific educational needs. I have even written detailed curricula for educational needs that I believe will change the way we teach and learn forever.

It is vitally important that you start all over again with the learning process. I am going to take you back to the place where all of the trouble really began, when you entered school. You had no real learning problems before then, because your parents, your first and best teachers, were using the best method of learning, but they really didn't know it. You will soon learn what your parents did to teach you and why it was so successful. You didn't have to worry about trying to learn intangible letters, numbers, words and symbols before entering school. You also had a great imagination as a child. You invented playmates and situations to keep your mind and your time occupied. As children, we get bored very easily and develop all kinds of make-believe situations to stay active and occupied.

School, unfortunately, dulls that great imagination. We don't like what we have to do and subconsciously click off our imaginations and similar skills to try and find something more enjoyable and fascinating. Unfortunately, this leads to far too much television, too many video games and passive activities. What differed in my development was that I didn't click off the imagination. I turned up the imaginative and creative juices even more by trying to develop tools of learning. As a result, Dr. Richard Watson, a good friend of mine who has tested some of my learning curricula, has said to me, "Jerry, you're different from the rest of us teachers because you think like a child." I consider that to be one of the greatest compliments I have ever received, and he meant it that way.

You need to start thinking once again like you did when you were a child. I will teach you how to stoke the childish fires of your imagination and how to have the wide-eyed anticipation you once had toward learning before school altered it.

CHAPTER 3

A Beginning for You

There are several points I want to discuss and have you understand before actually beginning to teach you. It is vitally important that you understand the principles behind **The Lucas Learning System**™ before any instruction starts.

The very best way to begin is with a test. Isn't that wonderful? I will be able to predict how you will do on this short test. All I want you to do is mentally answer yes or no to the following questions. Here they are:

1) _____ Yes _____ No
Can you describe what a giraffe looks like?

2) _____ Yes _____ No

Can you name the 23 uses of a hyphen in grammar and punctuation? You might be thinking, "I had no idea there were 23 uses of a hyphen." I find that English teachers even make that comment.

3) _____ Yes _____ No

Can you name the furniture in your living room in order from left to right around the room without being in the room?

4) _____ Yes _____ No

Can you name 30 of the 48 rules of capitalization from grammar and punctuation? You might be thinking the same kind of thoughts you did when I asked you about the uses of a hyphen, "I had no idea there were 48 rules of capitalization." In my research when writing curriculum for grammar and punctuation, I found that many rules were grouped together instead of separated for clarity and better understanding.

5) _____ Yes _____ No

Can you name the basic parts of the outside of an automobile from front to back? This does not mean that you would have to name any working parts in the engine or drive chain.

6) _____ Yes _____ No

Can you write the formula for the quadratic equation?

7) _____ Yes _____ No

Can you describe the appearances of most of the houses on the street where you live?

8) _____ Yes _____ No

Can you list the rules for using an apostrophe?

9) _____ Yes _____ No

Can you describe the basic contents and location of the items in your chest of drawers?

10) _____ Yes _____ No

Can you name elements number 10, 30, 9, 41, 16 and 5 from the periodic table in chemistry?

    I would say that you answered a yes to questions 1, 3, 5, 7 and 9. Why am I so sure? Because those were all tangible items that you have seen with your eyes. They are not intangibles that conjure up no picture in your mind. To understand the importance of that last statement, I must talk about the learning process of a young child. This child could have been you or me.

    When a child reaches the age when he or she is able to communicate with his or her parents, the first learning experiences begin. Parents are normally very eager to begin teaching their children and, in fact, become the first and best teachers the child ever has as I have already stated. You will understand why I believe parents are the best teachers a child ever has as this discussion continues. A parent begins to teach a child the only normal and natural way he or she can. Since the child can't read and doesn't know the alphabet, printed material certainly can't be used. All a parent can do is point to and identify tangible objects in the home and environment. In this process the following is typical. A parent will point to an object, perhaps a chair and say, "This is a chair. Look at it. This is a chair. Say chair." The child then looks at the chair, says what it is and is rewarded by the parent with a hug, smile or similar pleasantry. The child may not actually learn what a chair is with this initial exposure, but after a few other exposures and similar incidents the child will learn what a chair is. How does this learning take place? What actually happens can be explained in the following sequence. The child **sees** the chair, **recognizes** what it is and **registers** a picture of it in his or her mind. A miracle has just occurred, but the greatest miracle is yet to occur. What is really exciting is that the next time and every time that child ever thinks of a chair again, a picture of a chair automatically appears in the child's mind. The child **retrieves** a mental picture of a chair effortlessly and automatically. The knowledge of a chair has forever been locked into that child's mind. It can never be lost or forgotten for the rest of the child's life. The information has become **knowledge**, which is **the goal of all education**. This is the first and most important miracle of learning. It will be repeated thousands and thousands of times during that child's life. It is what I have come to call **Automatic Learning**™ , because the information is retrieved automatically.

I want to lead you through a typical sequential learning experience in the life of a child. A parent will typically do the following when beginning to teach a child to recognize animals, for instance. The parent could point to a picture of a cow and say something like this, "This animal is called a cow. Look at this picture. This is a cow. This animal has four legs. Do you see the four legs? We get milk from cows. Say cow. Look at this picture again and say cow again. What is this animal called? Cow, that is correct. Look at the picture and say cow one more time." This procedure will continue until the child learns what a cow is. What happens during this process? Once again the child must **see** the cow and **recognize** the cow, so he or she can **register** a picture of a cow in his or her mind. At the instant the child understands the identity of a cow a picture of a cow is automatically registered in the mind. Once the picture has been registered in the mind, the child can **retrieve** a mental picture of a cow by just thinking of it, because now the child knows what it looks like. Another miracle has taken place. The cow has become **knowledge** that the child can use. The bold words are **see**, **recognize**, **register**, **retrieve** and **knowledge**. These five words make up the process of learning that I call **Automatic Learning**™ .

In the next learning session let's assume that the parent shows the child a picture of a horse and asks what it is. I think we would agree that the child would call a horse a cow if asked to identify the animal without any explanation, because the child has never seen a horse before. The only animal the child knows is a cow. It is the only animal the child has **seen** and **registered** in the mind. The parent could then point to the picture of the horse and say something like this, "This animal is called a horse. Look at this picture. This is not a cow but it is a horse. This animal also has four legs like a cow, but it is different from a cow, as I will **show** you. We don't get milk from a horse. I also want you to see that a horse has a longer neck and a different shaped head and tail. People ride on horses to get from one place to another. They were used to get from one place to another before we had cars. Say horse. Look at this picture again and say horse again. What is this animal called? Horse, that is correct. Look at the picture and say horse one more time." The parent will probably point to a cow and a horse one at a time and ask the child to identify them. When the parent is assured that the child has recognized the difference between a cow and a horse, the lesson will probably end. Once again the child must **see** the horse and **recognize** it, so he or she can **register** a picture of a horse in his or her mind. Once the picture has been registered in the mind, the child can **retrieve** a mental picture of a horse by just thinking of it, because now the child knows what it looks like. Another miracle has taken place. The horse has now become **additional knowledge** that the child can use. Now the child knows the difference between a cow and a horse, because he or she has **seen** the difference and **registered** the differences in his or her mind.

I want to go through only one more potential lesson in this

series. I will make the assumption that next, the parent will teach the child what a giraffe is. The parent would point to a picture of the giraffe. If the parent asked the child what the animal was, he or she would most likely say a horse; of course, because it looks most like that animal he or she has already seen and learned. At that time, the mental retrieval storage mechanism, the mind, only has two animals stored in it to call upon to compare with the giraffe. The parent would probably say, "This animal is called a giraffe. It is not a horse. Look at this picture, and I will **show** you the differences. This animal also has four legs like a cow and a horse, but it is different from both of them, as you will **see**. We don't get milk from a horse or a giraffe, only from a cow. I also want you to see that a giraffe has a much longer neck and a different shaped head and tail." The parent would probably point out other differences that the child could **see**. The parent then might say, "Look at this picture again and say giraffe. What is this animal called? A giraffe, that is correct. Look at the picture and say giraffe one more time." The parent will probably point to each animal one at a time and ask the child to identify each of them. When the parent is assured that the child has recognized the differences between a cow, a horse and a giraffe, this lesson may end. Once again the child must **see** the giraffe and **recognize** it, so he or she can **register** a picture of a giraffe in his or her mind. Once the picture has been registered in the mind, the child can **retrieve** a mental picture of a giraffe by just thinking of it, because now the child knows what it looks like. Another miracle has taken place. The giraffe has now become

additional knowledge that the child can use. Now the child knows the difference between a cow, a horse and a giraffe, because he or she has **seen** the differences and **registered** the differences in his or her mind. The mental retrieval storage mechanism has added another picture to **retrieve** at any time. The **knowledge** that the child possesses has grown by one more tangible item. There is no limit to the amount of information that can be registered in the mind with pictures, because each tangible item is different from other tangible items, and each item has its own specific identity that conjures up its identity when it is thought about. It should be very comforting to realize that there is no limit to the amount of information that can be registered in the mind using your **photographic mental ability**. The only limit is the amount of time you are willing to spend developing and inputting information. You will be very excited when you learn how easy it is to do this.

What does this mean? It means that we have been blessed with the God-given ability to see pictures in our minds, and it is the only way for us to learn as children. As children we learn by the following already mentioned procedure. We **see**, **recognize**, **register** and **retrieve** information that becomes usable **knowledge** by **storing pictures in our mind**. We all have what I have come to call a **photographic mind**. Notice that I didn't say a photographic memory but a photographic mind. My definition of a **photographic mind** is simply the innate ability that we all possess to store and retrieve pictures of tangible items we have seen, recognized and registered in our minds. We actually possess an **auto-**

matic photographic mind, because the retrieval mechanism works automatically. This is what I now call **Automatic Learning**™. Once a tangible item has been learned, a picture of that item automatically appears on the **mental screen** in our mind when we think of it. Even blind people see pictures in their minds. My first blind student had been blind from birth, and I told him that I didn't think my systems would help him, because **The Lucas Learning System**™ was dependent on our innate ability to see pictures in our minds. His reply was, "I don't have any problem seeing pictures in my mind. I may not see exactly the same thing in my mind as you do when I think of an elephant, for instance, but I know what an elephant looks like to me from having one described to me and having felt a statue of an elephant. I have no difficulty seeing pictures and distinguishing one thing from another in my mind." I was pleasantly surprised, and he turned out to be an exceptional student.

Your photographic mind will enable you to learn faster and better than you ever dreamed possible. It is the only way we can possibly learn as a child and is, and always will be, the best way of learning anything. That is why our parents are our best teachers, in my opinion, because they teach us by using our very best learning gift. What they teach us in this photographic style is never lost or forgotten. It becomes **knowledge** that we can use throughout our lifetime. I will teach you how to use your photographic mind in remembering names and faces. Be encouraged, you have far more ability to learn than you ever imagined. I have far more confidence in you than you have in yourself, and you will learn that my confidence in you is warranted as you proceed through this book.

I haven't yet discussed the definition of a photographic memory. The two words actually define themselves. They mean to photograph and remember. Someone with a pure photographic memory would have the ability to photograph and remember everything the eyes saw. That person could look at page after page of printed material, for instance, photograph the information from the pages on his or her mind, and be able to recreate or retrieve that information by reproducing the printed pages on the mental screen in his or her mind. I don't believe anyone has that ability. I know I don't, but I have come closer and closer to that ability by learning how to use my photographic mind. Now it's your turn.

CHAPTER 4

Observation

Before teaching you the **tool of learning** you will use to remember names and faces, some further explanatory discussion is warranted. Observation is very important in learning. Observation is defined in the dictionary as the act of noting, perceiving or seeing. It is my contention that there is much more to true observation than this dictionary definition. **I think information must be registered on the mind before it is truly observed.** Let me prove it by taking you through a few of the observation drills that I use in my seminars.

You may be wearing a watch. If so, don't look at it until after I ask you a question and then ask you to look at it. Since you own the watch, you have seen it hundreds or even thousands of times. Try to answer this question about the number six on your watch without looking at it. Do you think the number six on your watch is a Roman numeral or the regular Arabic number six that we use in our number system? Please don't cop out and say, "I'm not really sure." If you aren't sure, guess. After you have decided which of the two you believe the number six to be, look at your watch to see if you were correct. Typically about 20% of you will have missed. Most of the people who miss realize for the first time that they don't have a number six on their watch at all but just a dot, dash or some kind of mark in the place where the number six should be. You may have been one of them. Certainly the people who miss have seen their watches many times, but true observation didn't occur, because **the information didn't register on their minds**.

I also ask people in my seminars to try to remember who is pictured on five, ten and twenty dollar bills. When I ask the audience to respond in unison by calling out the last names of the men pictured on those bills, it is amazing the names that are called out. But I do ask everyone to participate in the drill by calling out a name even if they aren't sure. I ask them to at least guess "Smith" if no other name comes to mind. You may not know who is pictured on these three bills. Certainly the people in my seminars have seen a myriad of these bills before, but many can't remember because the **information didn't register on their minds**. Their response is normally, "I haven't seen enough money to be sure. I guess I need to see a lot more of it." A pretty greedy excuse at best.

Let me ask you about a phone dial as I do the students in my seminars. Please don't look at a phone dial if one is near you. I want you to try to remember which letters of the alphabet are on the number one on a phone dial. In my seminars, I ask for a show of hands of the people who think the letters A, B and C are on the number one, and about two-thirds of the hands go up. Do you agree with them? If you do, you all are wrong, because there are no letters on the number one of a phone dial. The letters begin on the number two. There are also no letters on the zero, and two letters are missing. Do you know which ones? Most people can't answer these questions even though they see and use a phone almost daily. True observation doesn't really take place, because the **information isn't registered in the mind**, and the information isn't remembered. Are you beginning to agree that there is more to observation than the act of noting, perceiving or seeing?

One more observation drill should suffice to drive home my point. In a moment, I want you to read the large, bold words at the top of the next page. When you read the large, bold words don't speed read them and don't drag through them slowly. Just read them at a normal rate of speed to yourself. Don't read them out loud. Then after you read the words only once I want you to continue reading the rest of the information without looking back at the large, bold words. Do it now.

PARIS
IN THE
THE
SPRING

How many of the words "the" did you read? Almost 100% of the people in my seminars answer one "the," but they are wrong. I would imagine that you might have had the same answer.

Now look at the words again, and you will notice that there are actually two "the's" among those few words. What happened? Yes, you saw both "the's" with your eyes, because you looked at the words, and they were there, but one of them didn't register in your mind. True observation didn't take place. **To retain information it must be register in your mind**. To learn better you need a better "registerer." You already possess the necessary talent to have that happen. Your photographic mind will allow you to accomplish that task, but you need the proper **learning tools** to make it happen with names and faces.

CHAPTER 5

What Is Learning

Before discussing learning tools, I want to spend a little time discussing the actual process of learning. Learning is simply the process of connecting items of information together. Most learning requires the connection of **one** piece of information to **one** other piece of information such as a state to its capital; a product to its price; **a name to a face**; a word to its definition; a number in the periodic table to the element at that number; or an English word to its foreign equivalent when learning languages. I call this **One-On-One Learning**. I played basketball for many years at all levels of competition and played the well known **One-On-One** game countless times when practicing. That simply means **that one player plays against one other player**, and the best and most accomplished player wins the game. It would be far more difficult for a player to win if he or she had to play **Two-On-One, Three-On-One, Four-On-One** or even **Five-On-One**. When I was young, I used to be the One in Two-On-One and even Three-On-One games. I felt I would have to work harder and improve faster if I had to play against two or even three players at a time. You will be faced with similar kinds of seemingly overwhelming odds with certain learning situations, but be of good cheer. You can win in seemingly highly disadvantageous learning situations that require a Five-On-One or perhaps even a Twenty-On-One disadvantage. You may be introduced to as many as twenty people in a very short time span, but you will learn how to be a winner even against those staggering odds.

The Tools of Learning

There are **eight basic tools of learning** with some of them having adaptations or variations that the **Master Mind Mechanic** must understand and have at his or her disposal in his or her **mental toolbox**. He or she must also know which tool or tools to select for which learning problem or problems. All of these tools and their applications are taught in my *Learning How to Learn* book. You only need to know one of these tools to have success remembering names and faces. That tool is **The Sound-Alike Word System**. This tool is used to make intangible words tangible so they can be seen as easily as a cow or any other tangible object.

As an **Apprentice Mind Mechanic** for names and faces

you must learn how to use this tool efficiently and effectively. The basic purpose of all of these tools is to make the intangible tangible so it can be seen and easily registered in the mind.

I also want you to become an **ODD person**. I became a very **ODD** person. What do I mean by that? I mean that I was very **O**rganized, **D**isciplined and **D**iligent. The three letters in the word **ODD** stand for **O**rganized, **D**isciplined and **D**iligent. I will talk about organization, discipline and diligence throughout this book. A student in college, for instance, should return to his or her residence after a lecture and briefly organize lecture notes and class instruction to determine what needs to be learned. As a college student I was **organized** and **disciplined** because, being an athlete in a major sport, I didn't have as much time as other students did. I was also **diligent** to review the learning aids I had developed. I always arranged for interviews with my professors to learn how they conducted their classes. I asked if they tested from lectures or the textbook. If he or she said, "I test from my lectures only," I wouldn't even buy a textbook. I simply made sure I attended every class, took good notes and **organize**d my notes on a regular basis. As a result I was a straight "A" student my freshman year at Ohio State. You will learn later how I did this as you learn the application of my names and faces system. The important thing for me was to be **disciplined** to do a little each day so I wouldn't get way behind and have to stay up long hours when mid-term and final tests were given. I was also **diligent** to review on weekends. A businessperson must do the same thing. Lost notes, memos or correspondence not only can be embarrassing, but also can lead to business failure. I'm not talking about something that requires hours of application on a daily basis. I'm just talking about a little here and a little there on a regular basis. On a regular basis is the most important point. I will teach you how to be an **ODD** person as you learn how to remember names and faces.

CHAPTER 6

The Sound-Alike Word System

You have already read that the **Sound-Alike Word System** is a **tool** that is used to make intangible words tangible, so they can be pictured in the mind. Most of what we are called upon to learn is in word form, as are names, so this tool is vital in my names and faces system. Of course there are many words that are already tangible and automatically conjure up a picture in the mind. Those are the kinds of words that your parents and others began to teach you prior to entering school. Our problem is not with these words because they can be seen in our mind. Our problem is with intangible words. They are abstract or intangible and don't conjure up a comfortable picture in the mind. If you think of an elephant you can easily see an image of an elephant in your mind, but what about a pronoun? If a pronoun came to your front door do you think you would say, "Well, there's a pronoun. I haven't seen one of those in three or four days." I would think it is safe to say you have never seen a pronoun and wouldn't know how to go about seeing one. In that sense a pronoun is a **nothing**. By being a **nothing** I mean it has no tangible identity and conjures up no tangible picture in your mind. **It isn't a something** like a cat, horse, dog or tree that you can easily see in your mind.

It is difficult to learn that kind of intangible information in school. You had no idea what a pronoun was or looked like, so you attempted to go over and over the words that defined a pronoun until hopefully you learned the definition. To complicate matters, the words that defined it were also intangible. They were also a **nothing**. As a result, I say to people in my seminars, "So then, what were we trying to learn in school? **Nothing!**" The information was a nothing, since it had no tangible identity. My goal as a boy was to try to make intangible information tangible so I could see it. If I could **make a nothing a something** learning it would be easy.

A pronoun isn't a particularly hard problem, because it is defined with only a few words. When you had twenty or thirty rules in grammar to learn and had nothing to look at but intangible words, frustration set in quickly, and the joy of learning vanished in a hurry. The **Sound-Alike Word System** will give you the ability to make intangible words tangible, so you can see them like a cat, horse, cow or dog. Then they will be easy to learn.

The idea behind this system is to develop a new word that

will be tangible in place of the original word that can't be pictured. We know what a squirrel or a fox looks like. Each has its individual identity, so we can't confuse it with anything else. We can do the same thing with a **pronoun** or any other intangible word using the **Sound-Alike Word System**. We simply say the original word slowly and think of something that it sounds like that can be pictured, thus the **Sound-Alike Word System**. It doesn't have to necessarily sound exactly like the original word, but the closer we can come to the actual pronunciation the better. Look at this picture.

You see a picture of a **nun**. She is swinging a golf club. She is a very good golfer. As a matter of fact, she is a **pro** golfer. That makes her a **pro-nun** or a **pronoun**. Now you have seen your first pronoun. That picture does not teach you what a pronoun is. It is not intended to. It is simply intended to show you that you can see an intangible word that to this point never had a tangible identity in your mind. If you saw a nun walking toward you swinging a golf club you could now point to her and say, "There is a pronoun. I have seen one of those before."

When my children were young I wanted to make the learning process fun for them, so I developed a learning picture for the basics that they had to learn in school. I changed what was previously intangible and had no identity to tangible pictures that had an identity and had artists draw the tangible learning pictures, so my children could easily **see**, **recognize**, **register** and **retrieve** the information from their minds. **I changed nothings into somethings**. The ultimate goal was to make learning so much fun that they would be eager to learn more. They were, and in time I began to teach them my sophisticated learning systems and tools so they could become **Master Mind Mechanics** themselves. When they needed to learn the states and capitals, I developed and showed them pictures of the states and capitals that connected a state to its capital in a tangible picture. They were learning that each state and capital had its own identifiable picture like a cow, horse or giraffe.

In the picture on the next page you see a picture on an **ark**, like Noah's Ark, with a **can** in front of it. The ark is holding a **saw**. An **ark**, a **can** and a **saw** are my sound-alike words for the state of **Arkansas**.

The word Arkansas is no longer an intangible nothing. It has now become a something with a tangible identity. To learn the

capital it is necessary to see it pictured with the picture of the state. Look at the picture again, and you will see that the can is being used as a holding place, so the ark can saw a **little rock** in half. This pictures not only teaches that the capital of **Arkansas** is **Little Rock**, it also allows the student to see it in a tangible picture. **What was a nothing has been changed to a something that can never be forgotten**. The reason it can't be forgotten is that every time the student thinks of Arkansas after seeing and studying this picture the picture will automatically appear in the mind. It is impossible for that not to happen. That is the way God has made our minds to work. It is out of our control. Let me prove it more conclusively by asking you not to do something. It is easy not to do things. Doing something is sometimes hard for many people, but doing nothing is easy. Here is my request. Please do not see a zebra in your mind. That's right, do not see a zebra. You saw a zebra didn't you. It is impossible not to see any tangible item that you have seen and identified in your mind when you think of it. It's how the mind functions. It is out of our control. It is automatic. Like it or not, for the rest of your life, every time you think of Arkansas the picture of an Arkansas that you just saw will pop into your mind. You can't forget it now because you have seen it in a tangible picture.

I developed pictures for all of the states and capitals to make it easy for my children to learn them. Other parents asked me to help their children learn the states and capitals with the same pictures, so I eventually published a book of the states and capitals so others could learn them as quickly and efficiently as my children had. Something that had been such a problem in the past had become fun to learn. I continued to create more and more and more educational material to make the learning process for everything else as easy as learning Arkansas and Little Rock.

If you are interested in making learning fun and easy for you and your family, you will find a listing of a wide variety of books covering many subject matters listed at the back of this book. All of these books use The Lucas Learning System™ and are full of full color pictures to make the process of learning other material as easy as it was for Arkansas and Little Rock. Dr. Memory™ has done all of the work for you. There is no reason that you and your family shouldn't have fun when you learn. You can laugh and learn at the same time.

I must get on a soapbox at this point. If I had the attention of a million grade school children by satellite hookup and asked this question, "How many of you know what a cow is? Raise your hand if you know." "How many of you know what a horse is? Raise your hand if you know." "How many of you know what a bear is? Raise your hand if you know." What do you think the response would be? I don't think there is any doubt that every child would raise his or her hand on every tangible object I would mention, because they all would have seen them. But what if I asked this question, "How many of you know the capital of the state of Arkansas? Raise your hand if you know." Or what if I asked, "How many of you know the twenty-three uses of a hyphen? Raise your hand if you know." What percentage of the hands do you think might be raised in response to those questions? It is anybody's guess, but I think we could agree that the response probably would be that 100% of them would not know the twenty-three uses of a hyphen. Why, because they had never seen them tangibly like a cow or a horse. Their photographic minds easily retrieved a cow and other tangible items, but they had never even seen an Arkansas or the rules of using a hyphen. Hopefully school children all over America will learn the states and capitals and much, much more from Dr. Memory's™ fun learning materials.

Let's make another assumption. What if I showed the picture of Arkansas and Little Rock to those same children and taught it to them. If I had the same satellite hookup with the same one million children one week later and once again asked this question, "How many of you know what a cow is? Raise your hand if you know." As the week before, I think that every child would raise his or her hand, because they all would still know what a cow was. What if I asked this question again, "How many of you know the capital of the state of Arkansas? Raise your hand if you know." I think that we could probably agree that practically all of the children would raise their hands, because they had the opportunity to **see**, **recognize**, **register** and now **retrieve** a picture of an Arkansas. What a difference a picture makes! You have heard the cliché, "A picture is worth a thousand words." It certainly is when it comes to learning. It is my contention that every child in every school should have the opportunity to learn with these kinds of pictures. They would have more fun, look forward to the process more eagerly and certainly have more confidence and self-esteem, and they would learn.

The long-range goal would be to teach them to use learning systems to be able to create their own learning aids and become **Master Mind Mechanics** themselves. What if we fell somewhat short of that goal with every child? Motivation enters into each life and its activity. At least they would learn the basics of what have become known as the three R's. They would learn how to read, write and many other skills by pictures and could become a functioning member of society instead of a ward of society who ends up in prison or on welfare, because they didn't learn basic skills in school with which to become gainfully employed. This is not a pipe dream. It is what has consumed me for the last thirty years. Enough soap boxing, back to the job at hand.

You need to learn how to remember names and faces as easily as you just learned Arkansas and Little Rock. You will soon find out that you can.

CHAPTER 7

Names and Faces Made Easy
The System

I am sure you have heard people refer to others as old what's his name or whozit, because they can't remember a particular person's name. I heard people say it so much that I created a special character named **Whozit**™. I want to introduce you to my friend **Whozit**™ the elephant. Elephants have prodigious memory capacities, and I have also become world renowned for my memory and learning skills and learning systems. Since I played professional basketball, **Whozit**™ also is a basketball player. You see him pictured at the top of the next page as a basketball player.

Even though **Whozit**™ had a great memory he wasn't good at remembering names until Dr. Memory™ taught him his names and faces system. He was like everybody else who struggled with names and faces. He is pictured on the next page before he knew

how to remember names and faces. Does his look and comment remind you of yourself? He even had a bow tied around his trunk to try to remind him to learn how to remember names and faces.

As Whozit™ began to learn he developed more confidence in his abilities. He began to discover that he didn't need his bow as a reminder any more. Dr. Memory™ was giving him more and more confidence in his God-given abilities. He was discovering that he already had the ability built in. He just hadn't learned how to use it. You see him pictured in three different progress stages. He is thrilled with his newfound abilities, and so will you as you discover what he learned.

Everyone in the world is faced with the problem of trying to remember names and faces almost daily. We all meet new people on an ongoing basis. I have been asked to teach this skill more than any other subject matter, especially in the business world. It is a skill that is especially important for sales people who come in contact with so many people.

I'm sure you have said many times to many people, "I'm sorry, I remember your face, but I just can't seem remember your name." This statement is repeated thousands, if not millions, of times daily around the world. Have you ever wondered why people don't say, "I'm sorry, I remember your name, I just can't remember your face." The answer to this question is rather obvious. We all remember faces much better than names, because we see faces and only hear names. You will learn to see names as well as faces. When you can do that, you will be able to place a tangible picture for a name onto a face in a unique way, so that the face will tell you the name, because you will see a picture of the name on the face. You saw it done for Arkansas and Little Rock, and you will see it accomplished for a name and a face.

Many times over the years I have demonstrated remembering names and faces on well-known talk shows. For instance, I used to be a regular guest on *The Tonight Show* with Johnny Carson as well as the *Mike Douglas Show*, *Today*, *Good Morning America* and hundreds of others. As a guest of Johnny Carson I met people who were going to be in the studio audience that night. When I came on as a guest, Johnny would say something like, "I understand you met some people in the studio audience before the program started. Do you think you can remember their names?" I responded by saying, "Let me give it a try. Would everybody in the studio audience I met earlier please stand up." The whole audience, maybe 250 people stood up. I give them instructions by saying, "I am going to point to you and try to announce your last name. If I name your name correctly please be seated. If I don't, remain standing." I then proceeded to point to and name the last name of everyone in the studio audience. I've done that hundreds of times on television shows and in other places and have never missed a name. Why? Because the system, or plan, works well. You need to learn that plan and become proficient with it as well. If you do what I tell you, as a good apprentice should, you will become very adept and qualified rather quickly.

There are two basic reasons why people have difficulty with names. Faces aren't a problem, because they are seen and remembered rather easily. The first reason is that **people don't listen well** during the introductory process and they simply don't understand the name in the first place. If you happened to be in an introductory situation, heard the person's name, turned to take your first step away from the person, and then had me tap you on the shoulder and say, "Excuse me, could you please tell me the name of the person you just met?" I would venture to say that in probably nine out of ten times you would probably say, "I have no idea." Why? You simply didn't listen well enough to understand the name. I will teach you how to become a good listener.

Another problem is that you don't have a plan, and your mind is occupied with other thoughts rather than what it should be doing. The mind is an incredible mechanism. It can be used to our advantage, but at times it can also cause us problems. In the case of learning names and faces, it causes us problems, because it occupies itself with a variety of thoughts rather then an organized plan to remember the name. I'm sure you have heard of **absentmindedness**. A basic definition of absentmindedness is simply that **the mind is absent**. What does that mean? It simply means that, even though your body might be in one place, your mind is occupied with something else someplace else. It is simply absent from where the body is. Any teacher, including myself, can tell you that even though students' bodies may be in front of you, it doesn't mean their minds are. Mentally a student could be scuba diving in the Bahamas or snow skiing in Colorado. His or her mind is occupied with something other than what the teacher is saying, and what the teacher is saying doesn't register on the student's mind.

Hearing and listening are not one and the same. We hear with the ear, but our mind has to be involved with listening. If what is heard does not register on the mind, it might as well not have been heard.

It happens in the introduction process all of the time. You may be thinking of the next clever thing you want say to impress the person, or you may be looking around the room to see whom you could talk to next. You could also be checking out what kind of clothing the person is wearing or what kind of shoes or jewelry the person has on. It is obvious that your mind can't possibly be concentrating on learning the name under these kinds of circumstances. Why does this happen? Your mind doesn't have a plan to follow, and it wanders from one thing to another and doesn't understand the name to begin with. You need a plan, a plan that works.

My plan, Dr. Memory's™ plan, is a **three step plan**. The **first step has three key words** that must be discussed in depth. Those words are **Listen - Understand - Picture**.

The first key word is **listen**. You must listen attentively during every introduction. Most people aren't very good listeners.

When I began to teach myself how to remember names and faces, I found out I wasn't a very good listener either. Even though I felt I was listening well, I kept losing names. I felt I had to do something unusual to **force** me to listen better. I use the word "**force**" purposely. What this basically means is that we must kind of take our mind by the scruff of the neck and say, "**Stay here where you belong and listen to this name. Do what you are supposed to do.**" The mind will naturally wander if we don't **force** it to do what it should in introductory situations. I needed to find a way to **focus my attention**, so my mind didn't wander away from the job at hand.

The unusual thing that I began to do was **imagine that I had elephant ears during an introduction.** Not only did I imagine that I had elephant ears, but I imagined that I **wrapped them around the person as he or she announced his or her name.** In my mind, the only place the sound could go was directly into my ears, because my big elephant ears were funneling the sound toward my eardrums. This thought process forced my mind to think about nothing but listening. **I was totally focused on listening attentively with nothing else occupying my mind**. I began to understand far more names than I ever had before. It worked for me, and it will work for you, so you should imagine that you also have elephant ears during every introduction from now on. This thought will take your mind away from all the other things it could think about and force it to listen attentively to the name as it is announced.

You will discover that your ability to understand names will increase many fold as you put this suggestion into application.

The second key word is **understand**. That is the purpose for listening, to make sure you **understand** the name in the first place, and the third key word is **picture**. Under step number one there are six sub-points that must be discussed. I have already discussed point "a." They can be listed like this:

1) **Listen - Understand - Picture**

    a) **Listen** attentively with your elephant ears to make sure you **understand** the name.

    b)

    c)

    d)

    e)

    f)

As you can see there are five other points that must be discussed to fully develop step number one (1). Sub-points "a," "b," "c" and "d" are there to make sure you understand the name. In the perfectly working names and faces plan, sub-point "a" would work every time, and you wouldn't need sub-points "b," "c" or "d." However, as we all know, situations are not always perfect. There could be several reasons that you might not understand a person's name after they pronounce it for the first time. They could mumble, someone might tell a funny story at the same time the name is mentioned, and the laughter could drown out the name, or they could have an unusual accent, etc. If you begin to imagine that you have elephant ears as sub-point "a" instructs, you will begin to understand far more names than you ever have before, but you won't understand every name every time. If you understand the name after sub-point "a" you wouldn't need to use sub-points "b," "c" or "d," because point "a" would have accomplished its purpose. Remember that I said sub-points "a," "b," "c" and "d" are applied to make sure you understand the name. If "a" works, you don't need "b," "c," or "d," and you would move on to sub-point "e" immediately.

If you don't understand the name after point "a" for whatever reason, you must go on to **sub-point "b"** which is **politely ask the person to repeat his or her name**. There is no great revelation in this statement. It is painfully obvious, but most people don't do it. They don't understand the name and just carry on the conversation. Common sense tells you that you should ask the person to repeat his or her name. The very first rule of learning names, which is to make sure you understand the name, has been broken if you don't. Notice that I said "**politely**" ask the person to repeat his or her name. We should always be polite, but it is especially important to be polite during the introduction process. It is obvious that you want to make a good first impression on the person you are meeting, but there may be other reasons for this common courtesy. You should also **continue to use your elephant ears when the name is repeated**. Don't take those very large ears off until they have accomplished their purpose. If sub-point "b" works, you would skip sub-points "c" and "d" and go straight to sub-point "e." Remember once again, that sub-points "a," "b," "c" and "d" are there to make sure you understand the name. As soon as you do understand the name you will proceed directly to sub-point "e."

If sub-point "b" doesn't work though, you have to go on to sub-point "c." Before teaching this point, I want to discuss your reading habits to prove a point. I think I know what you do, or I should say don't do, when you are reading and come to a long, complicated word you aren't familiar with. No doubt, you don't put down what you are reading, find a good dictionary and look up the meaning of the word to make sure you know how and why it is used in the context of what you are reading. Not a chance! Most people don't take the time, or don't have the time, to do this with every word they don't know and understand. You just **zip** past the word and keep on reading. Another such word appears, and you **zip** past it. Then perhaps you **zip** past another and another. I call these kinds of words **Zip Words**. Just as there are long, complicated words that I call **Zip Words**, there are also long, complicated names that I call **Zip Names**. I actually call them **Zippers**. These are names with many syllables that can be quite difficult. The problem is that the person who is pronouncing his or her name knows it well, but you don't. He or she normally says the four or five syllables quickly, running them together. I say all of this to say that if sub-points "a" and "b" don't work, most likely you are dealing with a **Zipper**. I actually love **Zippers** and have a great deal of fun with them. It never fails that when I am doing a television audience of 250 or more people, forty or fifty people will say to me, "You'll never remember my name." The reason is that they are **Zippers**, and very few people ever understand and remember their names, but they are overjoyed when I remember and announce their names.

The whole point is, as I have already stated, if you have to go on to sub-point "c," you are dealing with a **Zipper**. Experience has taught me not to ask a person to repeat his or her name more than once. If I don't understand it after sub-points "a" and "b," I go straight to **sub-point "c"** which is: "**ask the person to spell the name slowly and listen for syllables**." Let me tell you what you might be thinking at this point. "If he thinks I am going to ask a person what his or her name is, not understand it and ask them to repeat it, and still not understand it, I'm certainly not going to ask them to spell it slowly and embarrass myself." I simply say this in response, "There is no way you can possibly remember the name, because you haven't yet understood it." You can't remember what you don't know. I'm never embarrassed, and you won't be either after you know **how** to do this. I have only taught you **what** to do to this point. When you learn how it is done you will be so excited and pleased with the results that you will look forward to doing it, because you will make a new friend in the process.

I'm going to call **Zippers** by name a little later, and they are going to be so excited that I remembered their name that they will never remember that I asked them to repeat or spell their name. Let me point something out to you. You think you might be embarrassed to do this, but **Zippers** have a special cross to bear almost every day of their lives that people with so called normal names don't have to deal with. This kind of situation isn't new to them, just you. It's incredible what some people will say to **Zippers**. People will scrunch their face up and say things like, "What kind of name is that?" or "What did you say?" These comments normally aren't delivered politely either. The reason I say all of this is for you to understand that you don't have to be embarrassed. Remember that the first word in sub-point "b" is "**politely**." I am always polite in introductory situations, not only because I think everyone ought to be polite, but I want **Zippers** to help me with their names if I need extra help. If you are polite and show interest in people and their names, they will be willing to help you. I will tell you later why it is important to listen for syllables. I didn't know I needed to do that when I first began to teach myself how to remember names and had to learn it the hard way.

Seldom, especially when you are first beginning to use this system and plan, will you understand the name after it is spelled slowly, so you will most likely have to go on to sub-point "d." If you do happen to understand the name after it is spelled though, you would skip sub-point "d" and proceed to sub-point "e." Assuming that you didn't fully understand it at sub-point "d" you would **pronounce the name back and ask if your pronunciation is correct**. You will discover a very good way to do this when you discover the **how** to do this and not just **what** to do.

You have a fifty-fifty chance here. You will either be right or wrong. That is a fifty-fifty proposition. If you are right, great, if you are wrong, there is still no problem. If I get the name right, fine, if I don't, I'm not that concerned. Let me tell you what invariably happens to me at this point, if I mispronounce the name. Remember that I have been polite to the person during this whole process. I even make it a point to show particular interest in what seems to be a very interesting name. Because of my polite manner, the person will be more than happy to help me by pronouncing the name once again, this time very slowly and very deliberately, so I can understand it. My plan will direct them to do what is necessary in order to succeed. Of course, if they had pronounced the name slowly and clearly at sub-point "a" in the first place, I may have not needed to fool with sub-points "b," "c," and "d." Finally I will have understood the name. A very important point that I want to make here is to make sure to do whatever is necessary to understand the name. You can't go on to anything else until this has taken place. You can't remember a mumble. In most cases you will never have to use sub-points "c" or "d" if you are using your elephant ears properly.

Our developing plan will now look like this:

1) **Listen - Understand - Picture**

  a) **Listen attentively** with your elephant ears **to under stand the name**.

b) If you don't understand the name, **politely ask the person to repeat it**, still using your elephant ears.

c) If you still don't understand it, you are probably dealing with a **Zipper**, so ask the person to **spell his or her name slowly and listen for syllables**.

d) **Pronounce the name back** to the person and ask if your pronunciation is correct.

e)

f)

Whether you would jump from sub-point "a" to sub-point "e" or whether you went there from some other sub-point, at **sub-point "e"** you should **use the name in your conversation to become more familiar with it**. The more you can say and hear the name, the more comfortable you will be with it. I will give you an example of the kinds of things I say a little later.

Now that you have understood and used the name, you need to move on to **sub-point "f"** which is to **develop a picture for the name so you can see it**. Any name can be made tangible. Some names are tangible in their natural forms. Do you think you could picture the name "**Fawcett**?" Sure you can. You can easily picture

a leaky faucet. What about the names "**Barnes**," "**Carpenter**," "**Rose**," "**Coates**," or "**Flowers**?" You can easily see a tangible picture for all of these names. Each of them conjures up a tangible picture in your mind automatically, because they sound like a tangible picture you are already familiar with. You will soon discover that any name can be made tangible.

The completed step number one (1) looks like this:

1) **Listen - Understand - Picture**

    a) **Listen attentively** with your elephant ears **to under stand the name**.

    b) If you don't understand the name, **politely ask the person to repeat it**, still using your elephant ears.

    c) If you still don't understand it, you are probably dealing with a **Zipper**, so ask the person to **spell his or her name slowly and listen for syllables**.

    d) **Pronounce the name back** to the person and ask if your pronunciation is correct.

    e) **Use the name in your conversation** to become more familiar with it.

f) **Develop a picture for the name** so you can see it.

I will come back to discuss the **how** of step number one (1) a bit later. You have just learned **what** to do. When you learn **how** to do it you will be very excited to put it into application.

Before going on to step number two (2), I want to mention a point that has already been discussed which is, most people are pretty good at recognizing and remembering faces, but they have trouble with names. **Step number two (2)** begins with the words **"pay attention to the person's face**." There are more words in this step, but I purposely cut the rest of them off to make some statements about the beginning words first. By paying attention to people's faces, I don't mean just a casual thought like, "Oh, that's a nice face. There is another nice face. There is another nice face. Ugh, look at that one." What you need to do is examine the face closely as the rest of the words in this step will make clear. You need to focus your attention on the person's face as keenly as your imaginary elephant ears caused you to focus on listening to and understanding names. The completed **step number two (2)** is **"pay attention to the person's face and select an outstanding facial feature**."

What do I mean by an outstanding facial feature? Obviously, I mean something from the neck up. You should try to find a feature that is so outstanding that it will almost jump off the face when you look back at it and say, "Yoo-hoo, here I am. You chose me." To do this, you have to fine-tune the face. It is kind of like tuning in an old-fashioned radio until it is perfectly clear. What could an outstanding facial feature be? You might notice something outstanding or unusual about the hair, hair style, hair color or lack of hair. You might select outstanding looking lines in the person's forehead perhaps, or you might notice big bushy eyebrows, very thin eyebrows, slanted eyebrows or unusually arched eyebrows. The person might have very large eyes, very small eyes or squinting eyes. You might think the nose is outstanding in some way. It might be quite large, bulbous, pointed, hooked, humped, square looking or pugged. You might notice very high cheekbones. The person may have puffy or sunken cheeks or a pointed chin, square chin or cleft chin. You may notice large ears, large ear lobes, a scar, freckles, dimples, a mole or a birthmark. The person may have a moustache or beard that draws your attention. What you are doing is examining the face and selecting some feature that will be prominent enough to draw your attention when you look at the face again. **Your attention is focused where it should be focused**. You are focused on the person's face, and your mind isn't absent from the job at hand. This system is designed to capture your mind and have it do what it should do to be successful. It forces proper observation and registration of information on the mind. You will become good at this fairly quickly when you practice as I ask you to later.

Step number three **(3)** is what learning is all about. This is where the connection takes place. The actual words in **step number three (3)** are "**connect the pictured name to the outstanding**

facial feature." I will teach you the nuances of this step as we proceed. In a nutshell though, what you will be doing is making sure you listen to a name, understand it and then picture it tangibly. After a facial feature is selected, you will attach the picture of the name to the facial feature in a unique way that you will soon learn. Later when you see the face you will see an actual, tangible picture of the person's name on the face. You will be quite excited when you learn how well this process actually works.

Before showing you some faces and teaching you how to attach names to them, I want to lead you through a couple of other applications, so you will better understand this process. First, I want to tell you how I handle step one (1) when faced with a zip name.

Let's assume that the person says the zip name so quickly when announcing it that there is no way it can be understood even using my big elephant ears properly. Sub-point "a" didn't work. I know right away that I am dealing with a Zipper. Immediately I say something like this, "That's a really interesting sounding name, but I didn't quite understand it, and I'd really like to know who you are. Would you mind repeating your name for me?" This is spoken in a very polite and friendly way.

Let's assume the person speaks the name very quickly once again so it can't be understood even though my big elephant ears really tuned in. Sub-point "b" hasn't worked. I now follow with these words, "Your name sounds even more interesting this time than it did the last, but I still didn't quite understand it. With such an interesting name you probably hear a lot of different kinds of comments, but I want to go the extra mile to make sure I understand your name. It's important for me to know you. Would you mind spelling your name slowly, and I will listen carefully and pronounce it back to you. If I mispronounce it maybe you could say it very slowly for me to make sure I understand it." Sub-point "c" is in progress. Sometimes the person will spell the name for me, and sometimes he or she will just say it very slowly for me to make sure I understand it without spelling it. I have never had a person at this point say, "No. I'm not going to help you." That doesn't happen because I have been very polite and friendly through the whole process. That doesn't always happen to Zippers.

If the person spells the name slowly to me, I listen very carefully with my elephant ears and try to distinguish as many syllables as I can. The more syllables I understand the closer I will come to the proper pronunciation when I say the name back which is sub-point "d." I will then say, "Is your name pronounced ---." I say the pronunciation that I believe to be correct. Once again, I have a fifty-fifty chance. I'm either going to be right or wrong, but I'm not concerned. If I mispronounce the name, invariably the person will say the name very slowly and clearly to make sure I understand it, and my goal of understanding the name is accomplished. They are much more apt to help me because of my polite and friendly manner with them.

The point is quite simple. I'm going to do whatever is necessary for me to understand the name. If I don't understand the name I can't go on. If the name had been "Coates," I would have never had to deal with sub-points "b," "c, " or 'd." I want you to know how to handle the very worst possibility. You will find out later how to make the worst possible scenarios easier and easier.

The second thing I want to do before showing you some faces and teaching you how to attach names to them, is lead you through an introduction that I had while doing the Mike Douglas Show a few years back, so you will better understand this process. When I do television audiences, I only do last names and not first and last names, because I can meet and remember more people in a short amount of time if I only do the last name. By the way, I don't ever get to meet the people in the seats where they will be seated during the program. I meet them in some kind of holding area like a big foyer or some other remote area. On the particular Mike Douglas Show being discussed, I asked a particular young lady in her early twenties what her last name was. I imagined that I wrapped my elephant ears around her to concentrate on her name as she announced it as I always do. I listened with great attention as step number one (1) **sub-point "a"** instructs. She blurted out several syllables that I didn't understand, so I immediately went on to **sub-point "b"** and politely asked her to repeat her name for me. You have already learned the kinds of things I say in this process, so I won't repeat them here.

She repeated her name and still spoke some unintelligible syllables that didn't register on my elephant ears. It was obvious that I was dealing with a **Zipper**, so I went on to **sub-point "c."**

After other polite and friendly words, the kinds of which I have discussed and you should duplicate, I asked her to spell her name for me slowly. As always, I was trying to develop a good rapport with this **Zipper**, so she would help me later if that became necessary. With my elephant ears at attention she spelled her name **F-O-R-N-U-R-A-C-K-U-S**. **Sub-point** "**d**" instructs you to pronounce the name back even if you are not sure of the pronunciation. I did, and she said that I pronounced it correctly. I began to **use the name in my conversation** as **sub-point** "**e**" instructs. Here is how the entire conversation unfolded. I said something like, "Is your name pronounced **Fornurackus**?" She said, "Yes, my name is pronounced **Fornurackus**, so I followed with, "Thank you Miss **Fornurackus**, I don't think I've ever heard the name **Fornurackus** before. What nationality is **Fornurackus** anyway?" Frankly, I didn't really care what nationality it was. I was just interested in using the name, so I could say it and hear it a few times to become more familiar with it. She replied with some sort of nationality, and I said, "Thank you Miss **Fornurackus**. How could I ever forget a great name like **Fornurackus**." As you are aware by reading this explanation, I heard or used the name several times. If you could hear it instead of reading it, you would know the exact pronunciation as I did.

But now I had the next problem. How in the world was I going to picture a **Fornurackus**? Let me assume for a moment that this name was the first **Zip Name** I had ever heard, even though it wasn't. I wasn't about to demonstrate on a national television show without knowing what I was doing. **Sub-point** "**f**" instructs us to

develop a picture of the name to be able to see it.

Assuming that **Fornurackus** was the first Zip Name I had ever heard I would have said something like this to myself, "I have to picture a **Fornurackus**. A what? There is no such thing as a **Fornurackus**. This system isn't going to work." I've told myself plenty of times during the years as I was developing my learning systems and curricula, "This thing isn't going to work," but I have never believed me! If you believe yourself when you tell yourself something isn't going to work, it won't. In this case, I said to myself, "No, I don't know what a **Fornurackus** is, but maybe I can picture part of that name, perhaps a prefix or a suffix or a syllable." I had hit on the secret of picturing Zip Names.

I'm going to have you help me develop a picture for this name. I want you to examine the last two syllables first. They are **rack-us**. Say it several times **rack-us, rack-us, rack-us, rack-us**. Think of something that it sounds like that can be pictured tangibly. It doesn't have to be the exact sound but just something close to the pronunciation and can be pictured. I thought of **rackets**, tennis **rackets**. Perhaps you did also. I had developed a way to picture the last two syllables of the name.

Now for the first syllable, which is pronounced "**for**." Its picture was obvious. I could simply see **four** of something. In this case, since the last two syllables were pictured as **rackets**, I pictured **four rackets**, **four** tennis **rackets**.

Since there was a syllable between these two sounds, I had to figure out what kind of four rackets they would be. The middle syllable is spelled "**nu**." What does **nu** sound like? Say it several times **nu**, **nu**, **nu**, **nu**. I wish you could hear me pronounce it. It sounded very much like the word **new**. So, now I had my picture for this **Zipper** which was **four new rackets**. You and I can picture **four new** tennis **rackets** as easily as we can see a cow, horse or giraffe. I had my secret of picturing **Zip Names**, and I began to practice the process to become better at picturing names. You will find out later how I practiced, and you will discover that my practice process and discipline that I possess will greatly benefit you.

Sound-alike words aren't needed for all names. I have already mentioned that some names are tangible and picturable in their natural forms. The name **Fawcett** was an example of one such name I used earlier.

Before I continue my discussion, I want to ask a simple question, "Do you ever waste any time?" Of course you do. I try very hard not to waste time. There are so many ways we waste time, but I believe television is one of the biggest wastes of time in the history of mankind. People sit glued to a television set hour after hour after hour, and I believe most of that time doesn't really accomplish anything constructive or positive in our lives. When I realized the importance of the need to be able to picture **Zip Names**, I decided I needed to watch less television and do something more constructive with my life. I began to spend some very exciting evenings away from television with a phone book in my lap. Wow, sounds like a lot of fun, doesn't it? What do you find in a phone book? Names, of course! I made it a habit to spend fifteen to thirty minutes a few times a week looking at as many names as possible in a phone book instead of watching television. As I pointed to a name I would say it out loud slowly several times. As I spoke the name slowly, I listened very carefully to the syllables in the name. By doing this, a picture almost fell out of my mouth for most names. If I had a problem with a name or a syllable, I always had a dictionary handy, so I could look up a possible sound-alike word that would work to help me picture the name. During this process, I began to develop standard ways to picture hundreds of names, and eventually, thousands of names. When I developed a standard way to picture a name I recorded it, so I could review it later. I also began to develop standard pictures for various prefixes, suffixes and syllables. Picturing names began to get easier and easier for me. I will list the standards I have developed later for your use. They will save you an immense amount of time. There is no reason for you to reinvent the wheel. They will be listed on the Doctor Memory™ internet web site for your use and review. You won't have to spend the thousands of hours that I did developing ways to picture names. The special auxiliary information code for the web site is printed on page 209.

      When I come to this point of instruction during my names and faces seminars I always hold my index finger and thumb together and say in a shrill, high voice, "I was able to learn how to picture names, because I had **a little bit of discipline.**" I then ask those in attendance to do and say the same thing. Several hundred people hold there index finger and thumb together and repeat in a shrill, high voice, "**A little bit of discipline**." I want them to begin to understand, as I do you, that all it takes to be successful in remembering names and faces is **a little bit of discipline**.

You see an artist's picture of me below holding my fingers together in this same fashion reminding you that you need to have **a little bit of discipline** to be successful. I am pictured on a fishing trip where I am fishing for more names.

Whozit™ is pictured below and on the next page in a library. In the first picture he is holding Dr. Memory's™ Dictionary of First Names. In the second picture he is holding Dr. Memory's™ Dictionary of Last Names. He wants to remind you that Dr. Memory™ has created these dictionaries to make picturing names easy for you. He has done the work for you. You will be able to access these dictionaries on his web site. The code for entering this section of the Doctor Memory™ web site is printed on page 209.

Now I needed to go on to **Step number two (2)**, which is: **"pay attention to the person's face and select an outstanding facial feature."** This step was very easy for Miss **Fornurackus**. I knew what feature I was going to use on her face before I ever heard her mumble her name. She had very puffy cheeks even though she was a thin, young lady in her early twenties. Those puffy cheeks seemed out of place on her face, and I knew that they would jump out at me every time I looked at her. She wasn't going to get rid of them and neither was I.

At this point I must talk about a no-no for facial features. You should never use glasses, earrings, hairpieces, braces or any other similar item when selecting a facial feature. These are items that may not be there the next time you meet the person. You are looking for an outstanding facial feature and not something attached to the face. You should also never use anything on the body. Some people have said to me, "I think I would use your height because that is very outstanding." Yes it is, but the next time you see me I might be seated. Use only facial features.

Now it was time to move on to **step number three (3)**, which is: "**connect the pictured name to the outstanding facial feature**." I use my common sense when making these connections. I want to do something to make the name as easy as possible to remember. Since her name was pictured by seeing **four new rackets (Fornurackus)**, I wanted to try to find something on her face that would almost automatically remind me of **four new rackets (Fornurackus)**. Since tennis rackets were the main theme of the picture for her name, I was looking for something that would work well with tennis rackets. She had **puffy cheeks** on an otherwise thin body, so it only seemed natural for me to imagine that she had tennis balls stuffed in her mouth. I thought, "No wonder she mumbles. I would too if I had tennis balls stuffed in my mouth."

I needed to develop a picture between **four new rackets** and **puffy cheeks**. I don't ever just place my facial pictures on the face. I want to see a lot of actions in my pictures. As a result, I make my pictures outstanding or unusual in some way. We naturally remember unusual or outstanding events or occurrences easier than run of the mill events or occurrences anyway. Lots of action in the pictures helps make the picture on the face more memorable.

I imagined I would help her out by using the **four new rackets** to knock the tennis balls out of her **puffy cheeks**. I imagined that I did that very thing. I saw myself walking up to her and, "pow," I knocked the tennis balls out of her mouth. It is very important to get as much action as possible into the pictures on people's faces. You might be thinking, "This is ridiculous. How could I possibly remember someone's name by imagining to knock tennis balls out of their mouth with four new rackets?" Regardless of what you think right now, it was practically impossible for me to forget her name, which I didn't, because every time I looked at her I saw myself using **four new rackets** to knock those tennis balls out of her **puffy cheeks**. It may sound stupid, but it works beautifully as you will soon learn when you meet a few people. You might also think, "I might call her **four new rackets** instead of **Fornurackus**." I don't make that mistake and neither will you when you learn the plan and get some practice with it.

Many people say things like, "I'll believe it when I see it," or "I'll believe it when I do it." You may be thinking the same thing. If you are, you are about to become a believer. I want to introduce you to a few people by telling you their names and showing you their faces. I will also lead you through the learning process for each face to give you some experience.

CHAPTER 8

Practice Makes Perfect

The three key words in **step number one (1)** are **listen, understand** and **picture**. That won't be a problem with these practice names and faces, because you will see the name spelled out, and I will give you a phonetic pronunciation if one is needed. The people you are about to meet are some of the many people I met on a particular television talk show. They are not made up names and faces to make the teaching and learning process easier. They are actual people that I described to an artist, so he could recreate them for my teaching sequences.

The first person's name is **Ponchatrayne** pronounced **ponch-uh-train**. A picture for the last syllable is obvious, a **train**. Say the whole name a few times and see if a picture comes to mind. I think it will. It is pronounced **ponch-uh-train, ponch-uh-train,**

ponch-uh-train. Have you thought of a picture? How about **punch a train**? That is probably what you thought of. We can easily see ourselves **punch**ing **a train**, can't we? Step number one (1) is completed.

Next we must look at the face and **select an outstanding facial feature**, which is what **step number two (2)** instructs us to do. Mr. Ponchatrayne's face is pictured below.

Look at it and select what you believe to be the outstanding facial feature. I always try to find something that will help remind me of the pictured name. The main picture part of this name is a **train**. As you look at his face try to find something that will almost automatically remind you of a **train**. If you can find something to remind you of a **train**, remembering the name will be much easier. I found something to remind me of a **train** as I studied the face, and I'm sure you will too.

I think you might agree with me about the outstanding facial feature. The **lines in his forehead** stood out to me. I imagined they were an actual railroad track in my mind. Step number two (2) is now complete.

Step number three (3) instructs us to **connect the pictured name to the outstanding facial feature**. Of course, we developed a picture for this name in step one (1). In this case, it is logical to think of the lines in his forehead as being railroad tracks, since a train is part of the picture for his name. As I said earlier, use your common sense to make the name as easy as possible to remember when connecting it to the face. Lines in the forehead and railroad tracks are a natural. Look at the picture of Mr. **Ponchatrayne's** face and imagine that a train is chugging down the tracks on his forehead. Then see it turning at a right angle and heading right at you. I'm sure you don't want the train to run over you, so **see** yourself **punch**ing **a train** back into his head. Imagine that you derailed the train and messed up the tracks. A tragedy took place on his face. Make sure to look back at his face and see the picture clearly, and you will see his name on his face. **Punch a train** will remind you of **Ponchatrayne**.

I won't keep mentioning the three key words in step number one (1), since you will see all of these names in print and be given a phonetic pronunciation to understand them.

The next person I want you to meet is named **Amato** pronounced **uh-mah-toe**. I want to introduce another possibility here.

Look at this name one more time, **Amato**. What tangible item comes to mind when you see that name even though it might not start with the same letter? How about a **tomato**? It isn't the exact sound, but it certainly is tangible and is close enough to the actual name to work. This new principle, or possibility, is that the picture for the name doesn't have to start with the same letter as the name. All it has to do is work! And, later I won't call this person Mr. Tomato, because I have decided that a tomato is going to be my standard picture for the name Amato. There are many standards I have developed that work extremely well for me, because I record them and review them from time to time, and their use locks the standard into my mind even more. Sometimes I use only a one or two-syllable standard in place of a four or five syllable name. As long as I know the picture for the name, as long as it reminds me of the original name and doesn't confuse me with any other name, it will work for me. For the name **Amato** we will see a **tomato** and know that we say **Amato** when we see a **tomato** on someone's face.

Next we must look at the face and **select an outstanding facial feature**, which is what **step number two (2)** instructs us to do. Mr. Amato's face is pictured at the top of the next page. Look at it and select what you believe to be the outstanding facial feature.

I think his **large eyes** are the outstanding facial feature. You may have selected another feature. Whatever facial feature you select as being outstanding will work for you, because that feature is the one that will jump out at you when you see the face again. But since this is a teaching sequence, we will use his large eyes.

Step number three (3) instructs us to **connect the pictured name to the outstanding facial feature**. We decided to use a **tomato** to picture this name, so we need to **connect a tomato to his eyes** in some unique way. I want to repeat a very important point here. Don't, I repeat, don't just casually place the picture for the name on the facial feature. You need to get as much action as possible tied into your facial pictures. Action will cause the picture to be more vivid in your mind. You will recall for Mr. Ponchatrayne, we got lots of action in the picture. Let's do the same for Mr. Amato, and you should do it for every face you ever learn. Look at Mr. Amato's face and imagine that he has two big, red, juicy **tomatoes** in his **eye** sockets instead of eyes. Talk about blood-shot eyes. He has a real problem. Now see his eyes blinking and tomato juice streaming down his face. Look back at his face and see this happening very clearly. Make sure to see the action.

The next person I want you to meet is named **Coates** pronounced **coats**. The sound-alike word to picture this name is obvious. We will simply see **coats**. The more you work with names and faces the more you will run into names that allow the sub-points in step number one (1) to occur almost immediately like it did for this name. This speeds up the process dramatically. The more names you know how to picture automatically, the better you will be at applying this system and plan. That is why I used to sit with a phone book in my lap now and then. I wanted to develop more and more standards for names to speed up the learning process. For instance, if you ever hear the name Ponchatrayne again, you will know how to picture it immediately. You have developed a standard for it. That name can now be pictured in your mind as quickly as a cow, horse or giraffe. That is why I have made my lists of standards for thousands of names available on the web site for your use.

Next we must look at the face and **select an outstanding**

facial feature, which is what **step number two (2)** instructs us to do. A picture of Mr. Coates's face is seen below. Look at it and select what you believe to be the outstanding facial feature.

I don't think there can possibly be any disagreement on this face. His **big ears** are without a doubt what we will use. **Step number three (3)** instructs us to **connect the pictured name to the outstanding facial feature**. We decided to use **coats** to picture this name, so we need to **connect coats to his ears** in some unique way. Let's imagine that Mr. Coates lives in Minneapolis. We know it gets very cold there in the winter. Let's also imagine that he is outside on a bitterly cold day without any protection on his ears. The wind is whistling, and his ears are freezing. Imagine that his **ears** put **coats** on to keep warm. Look back at his face and see this happening very clearly. Make sure to see the action of the ears putting coats on, and you will graphically see his name on his outstanding facial feature.

The next person I want you to meet is named **Berg** pronounced exactly as it looks. The sound-alike word for this name is obvious as well. We will see an ice**berg**. I said that we wouldn't call Mr. Amato Mr. Tomato, because we had decided that a tomato was our standard for Amato. The same principle will be applied with this name. My standard for the name **Berg** is an ice**berg**, so every time I see an ice**berg** on a face I don't say, "Hello, Mr. Iceberg." I say, "Hello, Mr. Berg." Once a standard is developed, there is no confusion. That is why I will instruct you later on how to build your skill at the proper rate before diving headfirst into applying this system and plan.

Next we must look at the face and **select an outstanding facial feature**, which is what **step number two (2)**, instructs us to do. Mr. Berg's face is pictured at the top of the next page. Look at it and select what you believe to be the outstanding facial feature.

I think we can easily agree to use the **long scar on his left cheek**. **Step number three (3)** instructs us to **connect the pictured name to the outstanding facial feature**. We decided to use an ice**berg** to picture this name, so we need to **connect an** ice**berg to his scar** in some unique way. Let's imagine that Mr. **Berg** was walking on an ice**berg** and slipped, and the point of the ice**berg** cut his **cheek**. Look back at his face and see that event happening very clearly. Make sure to see the action of the ice**berg** cutting his **cheek**, and you will easily know later that his name is **Berg**.

I am going to give you a quick review before continuing. Do not look back at any of the pictures of the faces during this review. You met a man with very distinguished looking lines on his forehead. Think of the face and the picture on the face. Do you know his name? I think you do! You met a man with very large eyes. Do you know his name? You met a man with very large ears. Do you know his name? How could you possibly forget it? You also met a man with a long scar on his left cheek. Do you remember his name? You did real well, didn't you? You should feel good about yourself. There are other things to learn like how to handle first names, how to remember names for long periods of time and more, but you are making progress, and we will get to those other principles later.

The next person I want you to meet is named **Fawcett** pronounced exactly as it looks, like a **faucet**. This sound-alike word is fairly obvious as well. We will see a **faucet**. This step was quick and easy again.

Next we must look at the face and **select an outstanding facial feature**, which is what **step number two (2)** instructs us to do. Miss Fawcett is pictured on the next page. Look at her face and select what you believe to be the outstanding facial feature. Don't be concerned when the feature I use may differ with your selection. This is a teaching session, and we will use my selections as a result. A feature you see as outstanding will work just as well in future applications.

I used the **bangs** on her forehead. They certainly may not seem to be very outstanding to you, but I want to use them to make another teaching point. If you spent some time thinking about using a lady's hair you might think, "Now wait a minute. If I use her hair, I may have a problem, because ladies change their hairdos, and the next time I see her she may have a different hairdo, and I won't know her name." Don't worry about that yet. I will show you how to avoid those kinds of problems when I teach you how to lock in people's names for as long as you want to remember them. Let's assume that you just met Miss Fawcett at a party. Your first goal is to remember her name for the evening's function. She certainly isn't going to run into the bathroom during the evening and cut her bangs off. They will be there for your use throughout the evening.

Step number three (3) instructs us to **connect the pictured name to the outstanding facial feature**. We decided to use a **faucet** to picture her name, so we need to **connect a faucet to her bangs** in some unique way. Let's imagine that her **bangs** are dripping water like a leaky **faucet**. They are going drip, drip, drip, drip. Look back at her face and see that action happening very clearly. See each bang going drip, drip, drip as you look at the face.

The next person I want you to meet is named **Sattlemacher** pronounced **sattle-mauker**. The sound-alike word for the first syllable is obvious. We will see a **saddle**. Think of the word **saddle**, look at the pronunciation of the second syllable, **mauker**, say both sounds together several times and think of a complete picture for this name. You may then agree with me that a **saddle maker** would work well. **Saddle maker** is my standard for the name **Sattlemacher**. Step number one (1) is completed.

The **next step** involves looking at the face to **select an outstanding facial feature**. Mr. Sattlemacher's face is pictured on the next page. When I first examined his face on the television show where I met him, his name became one of the easiest and fastest names I ever learned, because his facial feature matched his name so perfectly. Look at his face and select what you believe to be the outstanding facial feature.

I think we could agree very quickly on his **moustache**. **Step number three (3)** instructs us to **connect the pictured name to the outstanding facial feature**. We decided to use a **saddle maker** to picture his name, so we need to **connect a saddle maker to his moustache** in some unique way. I look for anything to make it easy for me to remember the person's name. In this case, what do you think I imagined the two sides of his moustache looked like? Since his name has a **saddle** as part of it. I imagined that he had **two saddles** on his lip instead of a moustache. As a result, his moustache almost vocally shouted back the word **saddle** to me. Look at his face and imagine the same thing. It is a good association that will help pop a **saddle** back into your thought process later. We have to connect the last syllable of the name along with

the first syllable, so I imagined that a **saddle maker** hung two saddles on his lip like a **moustache** to give them their final polishing
before delivering them. Look back at his face and see that picture
very clearly. Make sure to see the action of the **saddles** being pol-
ished by the **saddle maker** before continuing.

The next person I want you to meet is named **Pappas** pronounced **pap-us**. Say these two syllables a few times and think of
a possible sound-alike word to picture this name. I see a **papoose**
for this name. It isn't the exact sound, but it is close enough to
work, and a **papoose** is a vivid picture. Say **Pappas** and **papoose**
a few times to lock in the connection.

The **next step** involves looking at the face to **select an outstanding facial feature**. You see a picture of Mr. Pappas on the
next page. Look at it and select what you believe to be the outstanding facial feature. I'm sure your selection will be the same as
mine.

I think we could agree very quickly on his **puffy cheeks**. **Step number three (3)** instructs us to **connect the pictured name to the outstanding facial feature**. We decided to use a **papoose** to picture his name, so we need to **connect a papoose to his puffy cheeks** in some unique way. I imagined that it was cold outside, and Mr. Pappas stuffed a **papoose** into his mouth to keep it warm, and it caused him to have **puffy cheeks**. Look back at his face and see that event happening very clearly. See the two feet of the papoose kicking against one cheek and the head rubbing against the other cheek. Make sure to see the action of the **papoose** kicking and wiggling inside his mouth. No wonder he has puffy cheeks!

The next person I want you to meet is named **Kwiatkowski** pronounced **quiet-cow-ski**. Say these three syllables a few times and a sound-alike word to picture this name will fall out of your mouth. No doubt you already thought of it as you read the phonetic pronunciation. Here is a perfect example of a **Zipper** made totally tangible. Obviously, I see a **quiet cow ski**ing for this name. Step number one (1) is completed. Look at this picture. It pictures this zip name without a problem.

The **next step** involves looking at the face to **select an outstanding facial**. Miss Kwiatkowski's face is pictured on the next page. Look at it and select what you believe to be the outstanding facial feature.

I think we could agree on the **mole** on her left cheek. **Step number three (3)** instructs us to **connect the pictured name to the outstanding facial feature**. We decided to use a **quiet cow ski**ing to picture her name, so we need to **connect a quiet cow ski**ing **to her mole** in some unique way. Sometimes I use a cliché to help form my picture when it is appropriate. I'm sure you have heard of making a mountain out of a **mole**hill. Let's use that cliché here and see her mole growing into a mountain. What happens on some mountains? People ski, but we won't see people skiing on the mountain on her face. We will see a **quiet cow ski**ing on her **mole** mountain. Look back at her face and see that event happening very clearly. Make sure to see the mole grow into a mountain and see a

quiet cow skiing on the **mole** mountain. It has to be quiet, because it is a small mountain.

Now it's time for a test to see if you remember the names of these eight people. I will show you a picture of their faces again. When you see each face, do the following:

1) Look at the face carefully and recall the outstanding facial feature that was selected.

2) See the action picture that we connected to the facial feature.

3) Translate the sound-alike word for the name back to the actual name to recall the name.

CHAPTER 9

Long-Term Name Retrieval

I'm sure you were very successful remembering those eight names, and if they were real people who walked into the room where you are right now, you would know them by their last name. But what would happen if you didn't see them again for several months or even a year? Do you think you would know them? You may think so, but I don't think so. It didn't work for me. Once again, I recognized the face but couldn't recall the name. That bothered me, and I said to myself, "This thing isn't going to work." From my earlier discussion you know I didn't believe myselfe. I was determined to find a way to make it work for extended periods of time.

Before I teach you how to make sure you don't forget names no matter how much time elapses, I want to ask you to do something. Think of someone you know well who is not in the room with you. Think of them again. Are you able to see their face in your mind? I'm sure you are. You don't have to have a person standing in front of you to see his or her face. You can see it in your mind as easily as you can see a giraffe in your mind without having a picture of a giraffe in front of you. Knowing that, I began to think of how people normally remember names. It is obvious they meet someone and see him or her again, again, again, again and again. One of these "agains" they finally remember their name because of the repetition of seeing the person so many times. I thought, "Is there any way I could use my photographic mind capability to see people as many times as I wanted to without actually physically seeing them?" I realized there was. It seemed to me that all I needed to do was record some basic information about a person I needed to remember that I could review from time to time. Think of Mr. Coates, for instance. Can you see his face in your mind? Sure you can. From this idea, I developed what I now call **Long-Term Name Retrieval File Cards**. I began to write down and review the information necessary to recall the name. Before I owned a computer I recorded it on a file card that I could easily pick up and review.

On the next page you will see a picture of Whozit™ the elephant asking a file to retrieve a basketball for him that he threw into the water. You may think that names have been thrown into oblivion in the past, because you have had such a hard time retrieving them. Whozit™ and Doctor Memory™ will show you how to retrieve names from oblivion, so you can remember them for as long as you wish. All it takes to do it is **a little bit of discipline**.

I am going to use Mr. Berg as an example to show you what an actual log term name retrieval file card should look like. I will explain the use of the card after you review it.

Name - Bill Berg

Pictures - A dollar bill and an iceberg

Feature - Long scar on left cheek

Story - He fell on an iceberg and cut his cheek. He then reached into his pocket, pulled out a dollar bill and slapped it on the cut to stop the bleeding.

First of all let me point out what I did with the first name. As you know by reading the file card, I attached a picture for his first name, a dollar **bill**, along with his last name to the scar. With this information you could pick the file card up, review it at any time and see Bill Berg's face in your mind. You would have the first and last name recorded along with everything else you needed to be able to recall his face and name. It would almost be the same thing as actually seeing him again. As many times as you review the card, you will see him. This file card system works only if you are diligent to use it. If you develop and use a file card system, you will remember the people in your file. If you don't, you will lose their names. It's up to you whether you do it or not. What you need is just **a little bit of discipline**, and you will be successful.

I now store my name files on my computer. I have a

portable lap-top computer that I take with me when I travel. When I meet someone while traveling whom I think I need to remember, I put them into my name file in my computer, so I can review them anytime I choose. I have actually developed three different file systems. One is what I call a **current file.** This file contains information on people I have met recently and feel I need to review fairly often. Another file is my **permanent file,** which contains the information on people I had in my current file for a long time. After I feel I know them fairly well and don't need to review them very often I transfer them to my **permanent file** for review every four to six months. I will discuss another kind of file system later.

Sample name retrieval file cards are made available on Doctor Memory's™ web site so you can print them for your own use. The web site address and code to enter the area for downloading this information is printed on page 209. A sample of two cards for registering information about two people is printed on the next page.

NAME: _____	NAME: _____
SUBSTITUTES: _____	SUBSTITUTES: _____
FEATURE:_____	FEATURE:_____
STORY: _____	STORY: _____
OTHER INFO: _____	OTHER INFO: _____
SPOUSE & CHILDREN _____	SPOUSE & CHILDREN:_____

You will notice an area for **other info** and a section to list information about **spouse and children**. Sometimes it is important for me to list other information about a person that I might need to recall. I may want to remember that the person enjoys fishing or golf. Perhaps he likes to fly model airplanes. The person may have a title that you need to remember. He or she may be a doctor or judge or captain or whatever. Knowing this kind of information will help make a strong impression at a next meeting, and if you are in sales it may make a big difference in your success.

It is also quite important to know the names of the spouse and children in many circumstances. If you are to ask about a spouse and children by name you will definitely make a positive impression. I list this information so it can be reviewed along with the name of the person listed at the top of the card. If I remember more information about a person other than just his or her name, I have an opportunity to make a better impression at my next meeting with them. The reward far outweighs the small amount of time it takes to input and review the information. Remember to watch a little bit less television and have **a little bit of discipline** to review these cards and success will naturally follow.

You might be thinking, "I don't have time to keep and review file systems." If that is your thought and you act on that thought, you won't remember names for long periods of time. Remember that you only need **a little bit of discipline**, and you will be successful. It only takes a simple review from time to time to not lose names. Let me put your mind at ease by telling you first of all that it takes only a few minutes to review hundreds of names. To prove it, let me list only the names and facial features of the people you just met, so you can see how quickly their faces come to your mind. By doing this, it will almost be the same thing as meeting them again.

Mr. Ponchatrayne - Lines in forehead

Mr. Amato - Very large eyes

Mr. Coates - Very big ears

Mr. Berg - Long scar on left cheek

Miss Fawcett - Bangs on her forehead

Mr. Sattlemacher - Saddle shaped moustache

Mr. Pappas - Puffy cheeks

Miss Kwiatkowski - Mole on left cheek

You may have been surprised how quickly you went through those eight names. As I said before, it only takes a short period of time to review hundreds of names. I believe it is more than worth the small investment of time it takes to know people's names. The rewards far outweigh the investment of time. Anything worthwhile requires some sort of investment. The return on this investment will be worthwhile indeed. What you need to be successful is just **a little bit of discipline**. I will talk about first names in more detail later.

CHAPTER 10

Preparation for Business Meetings and Social Functions

If I know I am going to have a business meeting, I always call in advance and ask for an assistant, aide, secretary or associate to a person I know is going to be in the meeting if I don't already have a contact name for the company. I identify myself and mention the meeting I will be attending and ask for the first and last names of the people who will attend the meeting. If I don't understand a name, I will ask for a clarification, including a spelling of the name. By doing this, I have the names of those who will be in the meeting in advance of the meeting, and I can review the names to familiarize myself with them. I will know which first and last names go together as well.

I also ask if the company has a brochure with employees' pictures in it. If I get a positive response I ask that one be sent to me, or I make arrangements to stop to pick one up according to how much time I have before the meeting takes place. If I get the pictures, I will know the people before ever meeting them. I simply do everything in advance that I can to make it easier for me to be successful.

At every business meeting, always ask for a business card. That can be your file card if you don't use a computer. Simply turn the card over and record the necessary information after leaving the meeting. The name and particulars about the company are already on the other side of the card. Keep the card or cards in front of you during the meeting, so you can glance at them for a quick review of the name or names. After the meeting, put the card with the rest of your file cards for later review if you don't use a computer.

From time to time as my schedule allows, I teach seminars for large corporations. I have taught for many of the Fortune 500 companies. On occasions, just to have a little fun and drive a point home when I know I am going to be teaching over a period of several days at conventions, I have done something special with names. I ask the company to send me pictures of the people who will attend the convention, allowing enough time in advance for me to study the photos and learn the names. For one particular company, I asked them not to announce who the special speaker was going to be for the convention but just to say it was a mystery guest. They sent me the pictures and names of all those who would attend the convention. There were about two hundred people who would attend. When I arrived at the hotel where the convention was being held, I made it a point to get on elevators before anyone else. As people got on, I called them by name having never met them before. You know how weird people can be on elevators anyway. Sometimes people would just turn around and walk out of the elevator. All around the hotel comments like these could be heard, "You can't believe what happened to me. I got on an elevator and a very tall man I had never met called me by name." The response might be, "I can't believe you said that. The same thing happened to me." The hotel was abuzz with comments about this tall man who seemed to know everyone. They were pleased when I was announced as the special lecturer who was going to teach them how to remember names and faces.

I am going to give you a very good piece of advice for social functions that is very difficult for many people to heed. Get there early! Before telling you why this is important, let me tell you what will happen if you are the last to arrive. Assuming that Mary is the host, she will do the normal introductions when you arrive. She will introduce you to about twenty people in a few seconds. You won't have a chance to use the system. When this happened to me the first time when I was learning how to apply this system, I said to myself, "This thing isn't going to work." But as usual, I didn't believe myself. I said to myself, "I'm going to develop a way to make it work." One of the best ways to not get into that predicament is to arrive early, but sometimes being late is unavoidable. First I will discuss what I do when I arrive early before telling you how to handle late arrivals.

I want to be one of the first if not the very first person to arrive at a function. I don't want to be rudely early, but I do want to arrive shortly after the announced time of the function. If I happened to be the first to arrive, Mary would have nobody else to introduce the next guest to but me. When she makes the introduction, I immediately begin to apply the three-step plan and use my big elephant ears. I make sure I understand the first and last name and use the names in my conversation. When I walk away from the person, I pull a little notebook out of my pocket. I always have something with me on which to write, especially if I know I'm going someplace where I will be meeting people for the first time. After I walk away, I write the person's name down in my notebook, so I have a record of it. Then I look back at the person and complete the steps in my plan. I lock a picture of the name onto the facial feature I selected and see it very clearly with lots of action. I see the action happening over and over again as a review.

When the next person comes, I make it a point to meet them as quickly as possible. **Whap**! I wrap my elephant ears around them and start the procedure all over again. I walk away, record the name in my notebook, look back at them and develop my feature and picture. When I do that, I then review the pictures on the faces of both of the people I have met by looking back at them. I will know them better and better as my review continues. I continue the same process as other people arrive. By the time the last person arrives, I will know everyone. Not only that, I will have recorded all of their names, so I can develop a name file card for them if I think it is important for me to remember their name for a long period of time. This is a personal decision that must be made by you. I have to make that decision myself for the people I meet. If I feel I will need to know your name in the future you are added to my name retrieval file. If I don't feel I might need to know you in the future your name will not be added.

Now let me go back to the late arrival scenario. You arrive last and are introduced to far too many people in far too short a time period to even understand the names, much less try to remember them. Is all lost? No, but it will take some special effort on your part to learn everyone's name. I go back to each person one at a time and say something like this, "I'm sorry, Mary introduced us so quickly that I didn't understand your name, and I would really like to know you. Could you please tell me your name again?" **Whap**! I wrap my big elephant ears around that person and begin to follow my plan. After the conversation is complete, I walk away get my notebook out and record the name. Then I look back to find a feature if I haven't already found one and complete the plan with an action picture on the face. I continue to go back to one person at a time following the same procedure. It will take a lot longer, but it will still work. You would be amazed how many trips to bathrooms I take to review my name list to make sure I know them. If I was watched closely some guests might think I had some sort of problem. Actually I do. I arrived late and had a lot of work to do to learn everyone's names.

CHAPTER 11

Building Your Skill

You will learn more of my system soon, but as I learned more and more about how to remember names and faces, I realized it was important to build my skill level to improve my ability. I had to find the best way of practicing to build my skill. Whozit™ is pictured on the next page to remind you that you also need to build your skill level a block at a time to reach your goal of being a professional at remembering names and faces.

I became a pretty good basketball player, because I practiced more than anybody else did. I used to practice twelve or fifteen hours a day when I was a boy. The lights went out at the local park basketball court at eleven p.m. in the summer, so I would go home after that and shoot baskets by moonlight until my mother or father chased me in at two or three in the morning. I didn't have any grandiose ideas of becoming a great player. I just played because I loved the game. I became good at remembering names and faces in a mere fraction of the time that it took me to become good at basketball. As a matter of fact, the very first time I ever demonstrated remembering names and faces was on the *Johnny Carson Show.* I had never even demonstrated at the local PTA or anywhere else, but I knew I could meet and remember hundreds of names. How did I know? I had practiced. I had a plan that I thought would give me the experience I needed to be successful, and I completed it without really ever officially meeting anyone. How was this possible?

I am going to repeat a question I have already asked. Do you ever waste any time? A silly question, of course. Everybody wastes time. I felt I could become good at remembering names and faces if I began to redeem some of the time that I normally wasted. I thought to myself, "Where do I normally and regularly waste time where people are around? Many times I sit with nothing to do while waiting on a meal to be delivered at a restaurant. I also waste lots of time in layovers in airports." These were only a couple of examples of wasted time where people were around that I felt I could use to my advantage. My idea was simple enough. I would write down twenty or so names on a piece of paper or card after reviewing some names in a phone book in the evening. This would give me practice at developing sound-alike words for names.

The next day I placed the piece of paper or card in a pocket. If I happened to go to a restaurant where I had to wait on a meal to be delivered, I pulled the piece of paper or card out of my pocket and started my plan. I looked around the restaurant, selected a person, chose an outstanding feature on the face and attached the picture for the first name on the list to that facial feature. I started by using easy last names. I knew I had to go slowly at first and use simple easy-to-picture names. After I saw that action picture clearly, I chose another person, selected an outstanding feature on that face and attached the picture for the second name on my list to that feature. Before going on to the next person, I reviewed persons one and two briefly to see each action picture more clearly. Then I chose another person and started the process all over again. I continued the practice session until my meal was delivered. If service was slow, I wasn't too upset, because I was busy practicing. It didn't matter to me that I wasn't using that person's actual name. I was practicing. That was all that mattered. I probably would never see them again anyway, and I certainly wasn't going to put them on a name file to remember fictitious names for a long time.

I continued to do this on a regular basis and got better and better and faster and faster. I gradually used more difficult and more complicated names, and it still worked. I was learning to remember names and faces in a similar way that I learned to be a good basketball player. As a young inexperienced basketball player, I always tried to play with players who were bigger and stronger than I, in order to gain experience and put more pressure on my skills. I gradually did the same thing with names. After a while, twenty names were too easy. I got to the point where I could learn them very quickly. You never really know what you can do until you try. Unfortunately, some people never try much of anything with their abilities and never learn of life's potentials. What you need is just **a little bit of discipline**.

I wanted to start learning more names and put more pressure on myself. I got an idea. I thought, "I'm in airports a lot with nothing to do, and there are always hundreds of people around. Why not develop some fold out cards with hundreds of names on them that I can use in airports. I can meet as many people as I want there." I started to do just that. I would go from one gate to another practicing selecting features and connecting names to the features especially when there was a weather delay for all passengers. When I met everyone in that gate and had properly reviewed them, I would go to another gate to meet more people. After I met as many people as my fold out cards had names, I would walk around the airport seeing how many people I knew. I began to increase the numbers and decrease the time spent on each face to see how far I could push the limits. I found my comfort zone by putting this kind of pressure on myself. I found out what I could accomplish and how fast I could accomplish it. I never would have known, nor would I have had the confidence to demonstrate my ability on television shows had I not participated in practice sessions. I called these cards my **Skill Builder Cards**, simply because they gradually built my skill level to a higher plateau. I have made these **Skill Builder Cards** available to you on Doctor Memory's™ web site. When you go to the site and use the auxiliary information code on page 209 you can print them out for your own use.

A sample card from the **Skill Builder** series of cards for the first practice day appears on the next page. The front of the card is on the left, and the back of the card with the instructions for its use is on the right. As the cards progress the names get longer and more complicated. You will also find lists of male and female first names to attach along with the last names as you progress through the series and improve your skills. These cards are very helpful for increasing your knowledge for standards for both first and last names as well. First names will be discussed in more detail later in this book.

PRACTICE LIST FOR DAY #1
DON'T FORGET TO PRACTICE SELECTING FEATURES ON EVERYONE YOU SEE

CAMPBELL — SOUP (CAMP-BELL'S SOUP)
HYDE — HIDE SOMETHING OR PLAYING HIDE & SEEK
COHN — AN ICE CREAM CONE
ROSE — A ROSE (THE FLOWER)
WATERS — RUNNING WATERS
GOFF — GOLF (PLAYING GOLF)
TAYLOR — A TAILOR
PECK — PECK ON SOMETHING LIKE A WOODPECKER
WADE — WADE IN WATER
PEACOCK — A PEACOCK (THE BIRD)
BOOTH — A RESTAURANT BOOTH
HARPER — ONE WHO PLAYS A HARP OR JUST A HARP FOR SHORT
BELL — A BELL (I USE THE LIBERTY BELL)
WALKER — A BABY WALKER A PERSON WHO WALKS A LOT
PAYNE — A PAIN (ACHE) OR A WINDOW PANE
PRICE — A PRICE TAG
LYONS — LIONS
WRIGHT — TO WRITE WITH A PEN OR PENCIL
LYNCH — TO LYNCH OR HANG SOMEONE
REED — READ A BOOK OR A GRASS REED

RULES FOR USING PRACTICE LISTS

1. LEARN SUBSTITUTES THE NIGHT BEFORE
2. TAKE THIS CARD WITH YOU
3. USE THIS CARD
4. SELECT A FEATURE ON A PERSON
5. ASSOCIATE THE TOP NAME TO THEIR FACE
6. SELECT A FEATURE ON ANOTHER PERSON
7. ASSOCIATE THE SECOND NAME ON THE LIST TO THEIR FACE
8. REVIEW FACES ONE AND TWO
9. CONTINUE TO SELECT FEATURES AND USE NAMES ON THIS LIST
10. REVIEW ALL THE FACES AFTER USING EACH NEW NAME
11. FROM TIME TO TIME DURING THE DAY TAKE THIS CARD OUT AND TRY TO RECALL THE FACES THAT GO WITH THE NAMES

COMMENTS _____
_____
_____
_____
_____
_____
_____

There are also other ways for you to build your skill without actually meeting people. You can go through catalogs and select facial features and give names to clothing models in the catalog. Then simply leaf through the catalog to see if you remember the names that were given to each model. There are a variety of catalogs that can be used for this purpose.

As I was building my own skill level Johnny Carson's producer called and said, "Jerry, Johnny wants to have you back on the show next week. What can you do this time?" I replied, "I will meet everybody in the studio audience before the program, learn their names, have them stand up at a later time, point to them, name their names and ask them to be seated if I name their name correctly." He replied, "You can't do that." I shot back, "Oh, yes I can!" He once again said, "No you can't. What producer can I call to verify that you can do this?" I answered honestly, "I have never demonstrated my ability anyplace, but I know I can do it. I have practiced." He said, "Jerry, there will be 250 or more people in that audience." I confidently said, "I don't care if there are 500. I will name them all." Maybe I had overstepped my present confidence level just a bit, but I wanted to sound convincing. The next thing he said was, "Jerry, even if you can remember them, it will take you too long to name them." I said, "Oh, no it won't. I will name them all in a couple of minutes." I didn't really know if I could do this or not, but I sure wanted to try. Then I said, "I haven't failed Johnny yet in any of the other demonstrations, have I?" I had been Johnny's guest several times. I had been on and demonstrated my alphabetical spelling. I had memorized a full 100 page current *Time* magazine and had Johnny test me on it among other things. Whatever I said to him worked, because he agreed to give me a shot at remembering the names in the audience. The night of the show I met over 250 people, had them all stand up and rattled their last names off quickly and accurately without missing any.

It was a big hit, but it wasn't really done that night. It was done in all of those restaurants, public buildings and airports in the many practice sessions that gave me the confidence and experience to even try to do something like that. I have demonstrated my ability to do this on hundreds of television shows and in various other places since that time. It always amazes people, but it is so easy for me because of my experience. The most people I have met and remembered at one time is seven hundred. I'm sure I could do a thousand if I had the time. One of the most fun times of demonstration I ever had was when I did an audience of about 150 Japanese people in Hawaii. Almost every name was one that I had never heard before and I was challenged. I named them all and felt more confident than ever afterwards. It was like trying to find a bigger and better player to play against to improve as a young basketball player. I welcomed the challenge and passed with flying colors.

Do you want to get good at remembering names and faces? If your answer was yes, start practicing. Have **a little bit of discipline**. I have developed thousands of standards for first and last names. They will help speed up your learning process. I also have supplied a complete set of **Skill Builder Cards** for your practice purposes. You never know what you might accomplish until you try. It is very important to note that I also practiced my plan with every regular introduction I encountered. I wasn't just **using Skill Builder Cards**. Actual and real introductions put the finishing touches onto my abilities. You can do the same by having **a little bit of discipline**.

When applying this system, your mind will have a definite three step plan to follow, so it shouldn't wander away from the job at hand. You need to learn to discipline your mind and make it do what it should do instead of wandering all over the place from idle thought to a non-productive idle thought.

It is important to not try to exceed your capabilities. I met and talked with a pastor recently who had read one of my Bible memory books. He said, "Jerry, I know your systems work, because I have applied them in many areas in my life. But I don't know your names and faces techniques, and I'm having trouble remembering the names of people in my new church. I have recently moved to a new church of several hundred people. I try to remember their names as they leave the church, but it isn't working." It was obvious to me why it wasn't working. He didn't know how and had to meet too many people in too short a time. It is like arriving late at a function and being introduced to twenty or more people in a very brief time frame. It won't work unless you find a way to make it work.

I took the time to teach him my names and faces system and

said, "Sam, I'm going to tell you how to solve your problem. Ask an associate who has been at the church longer than you and who may sit next to you on the platform to point out people in the congregation. Pay particular attention to them during your spare time during the service and make a point to contact them after the service and spend a little time talking with them. Then go back and make up a name card on them for your review time. This way you will at least learn a few new people each week instead of being confused with hundreds of people."

I then asked if the church had a church directory. He didn't know. When he inquired one was made available to him. Low and behold, not only did the directory contain all the names of the members, it also contained their pictures. His problems were over. He had the ultimate name file system. What could be better than pictures along with the names and other information you record? He began to study the church directory and called me later to tell me about his success. You should also ask questions. You never know what you might find to help you. If it is at all possible to add pictures to your name file systems, do it! When pictures are available it becomes the ultimate file system.

I have a unique but fun problem with names and faces. Millions of people have seen me demonstrate remembering whole audiences on television programs, and I have taught literally hundreds of thousands of people in seminars. As a result, people may recognize me, tap me on the shoulder, and when I turn around they ask, "Who am I?" About ninety-nine out of a hundred of those people I have never met in my life. They just want to have a little fun, and I enjoy talking to people, so I respond, "If you don't know who you are, how in the world do you expect me to know? Where did I teach you?" I end every one of my "How to Remember Names and Faces" seminars with this suggestion, so more and more people tap me on the shoulder and ask me that question. If you ever see me, come up to me and ask the same question, and I will respond with, "If you don't know who you are, how in the world do you expect me to know? Where did I teach you?" You can reply, "I read your *Names and Faces Made Easy* book."

CHAPTER 12

What Ifs

When various people first begin to think about using this system and plan, they start thinking about what I call **what ifs**, and many of them are legitimate thoughts. For example a typical thought might be: "**What if** I meet twenty-five people and select noses as the outstanding feature on five different people. Will I get confused because I am using five noses?" The answer is absolutely not. I thought the same thing when I began to perfect this system, but I found out very quickly when that there was no confusion because of the review process that easily eliminated any potential confusion. When you begin to practice, you will find this out for yourself. When I have demonstrated doing audiences of 250 or more people, I may choose twenty-five or more noses from a group of people. When doing these demonstrations, I do an incredible amount of quick mental review. After meeting four or five people, I will step back and review by looking at their faces again to recall the action picture and their names. This process helps me lock the names in more and more securely. This is the same process I told you to use at social functions. By the time I get to the last of 250 or so people, I may have reviewed the first few people a hundred times each. Mental reviews go very quickly after you get experience. Not only that, I continue to review faces over and over again as long as I possibly can until the people are directed to be seated in the studio audience. Even after they are seated, I continue to look at them and review their faces. If for some reason a name slips away, I simply walk back to the person and ask them to repeat the name to me again. It is absolutely mandatory for these kinds of demonstrations for the group of people to be in the same place for an extended period of time, so I can take part in this absolutely critical review process. I have had as little as an hour to meet and remember as many as 200 or more people. Without my airport practice, demonstrations like that would have been impossible. Your own review process will eliminate this **what if**, and you certainly won't have to meet and remember hundreds of people at a time.

A very typical question that always comes up is: "**What if** I meet twenty-five people and four or five of them have the same name, such as Smith. Will I get confused?" Once again, the answer is absolutely not. My standard picture for the name **Smith** is a black**smith** hammer. Let's assume that one man named **Smith** had large, bushy eyebrows. I would probably imagine myself using a blacksmith hammer to shape his eyebrows into a horseshoe. Let's assume another man named **Smith** had a flat nose. I would probably imagine that I used a blacksmith hammer, hit him in the nose and flattened it. I would continue to use a blacksmith hammer for every person named **Smith** in that audience or group of people, because that is my standard for picturing the name **Smith**. That will never change. A blacksmith hammer is always **Smith** as a cow is always a cow. You don't see a giraffe in your mind when you think of a cow, because a cow has its own individual, distinctive identity that always recalls the same picture. That is and should always be the same for names. **Smith** is always a blacksmith hammer. I don't want to confuse myself.

Now back to the original point. Don't forget about the continual review process that I go through when learning an audience or large group of people. When I see the man with large, bushy eyebrows again, I will see that I used a blacksmith hammer to shape them into a horseshoe and know his name is **Smith**. When I see the man with the flat nose again, I will just as readily know that I used a blacksmith hammer to flatten his nose, and I will know that his name is **Smith** as well. Experience will show you that this is the case. You will not be confused because of the review process. Your review process will eliminate this **what if** as well.

Another typical question is, "**What if** I meet twins, will I get confused?" What happens with most people is that they look at twins hurriedly and say something like, "Isn't it amazing. They look just alike." Well, I have never seen a set of twins that look exactly alike even if they are so-called identical twins. I have always been able to find one small characteristic on one of them that the other one doesn't have. One may have a small scar that the other one doesn't, or one may have a small mole or blemish of some kind that the other one doesn't have. To find something like this, it takes some careful examination of the faces. A quick glance, like most people give, won't suffice in this situation. After I find what I'm looking for, I develop my picture on the twin who has the prominent feature first, and the other guy has to be the other one with the other name. By careful examination this **what if** will also be eliminated.

Another typical question is, "**What if** I meet someone, learn their name and develop a name file card for review and their facial feature changes? What if they had a large, bushy beard and later shaved it off. Will I get confused?" Yes, it is very possible that you might not know that person when you see them again. But, you will have a legitimate excuse because of the change of feature. It is entirely possible that his close friends might not recognize him. In cases like these, you must be observant to find a new outstanding facial feature. You must go back to your name file card and change the section on facial feature. Maybe you noticed a mole or small birthmark where the beard used to be. Note the new facial feature as well as the fact that he shaved off his beard as you change the information in your name file system. I would put that information in my current file if it had been transferred to a permanent file to make sure it got some special attention in the next few days and weeks.

Similar occurrences have happened to me more than once. In one particular case, I had a friend named Tank Spangler in my hometown of Middletown, Ohio when I was growing up. Tank got his nickname, because he was large and overweight, somewhat like a tank. It served him well as a high school football player, but the extra weight wasn't healthy even for a teenager. I had known Tank for years when I left to attend Ohio State University. When I came home for the summer, I happened to be in a restaurant having a sandwich at a counter. The person seated next to me said, "Hello, Jerry, how are you doing?" I politely replied, "Fine thank you," and said some other polite words. Many people whom I didn't know knew me because of basketball. He kept talking to me and began to mention some things that a stranger should have no knowledge of. I finally said, "Excuse me, how do you know about all these things? I don't even know you." He replied, "Of course you do, Jerry. We have known each other for years. We grew up together." I followed with, "There must be some mistake here. I don't ever remember meeting you." He laughed and said, "Jerry, I'm Tank Spangler, and I have lost over a hundred pounds. That's why you don't recognize me." Was I ever surprised and happy! I was not only happy to see a good friend again, but I was happy for Tank and his weight loss. Here is an example of someone I had known well for many years but didn't recognize because of the tremendous change in his appearance. I had a legitimate excuse. I say all of this to make the point that sometimes, no matter how diligent you are a feature may change so much that you don't know the person. That certainly doesn't happen very often, and it certainly isn't an excuse for not using this system. All **what ifs** have an answer that will make them work.

Whatever kinds of questions you come up with will be answered when you begin to get experience in the actual application of practice with your own **Skill Builder Cards**. Experience is always the best teacher.

CHAPTER 13

Travel Files

Whozit™ is pictured on the next page to remind you that you also need to create travel files to reach your goal of being a professional at remembering names and faces.

Travel Files are simply files that are arranged to help me be more prepared to know names when I travel. These files can be arranged one of several ways. You can have names listed by city, and these names can be reviewed when you are preparing to travel to that city. This review will help refresh your memory of the people you have met and should know in that city. The files can also be arranged by company name or any other category that is important to you.

For instance, I have done a lot of teaching in churches. I teach, among other things, how to learn the Bible. Scripture memory is very important to me and to many other people. As a result, one of my name arrangements is by church. It is a simple matter for me to review the names of the people I met at that church if I happen to visit it again. You must determine which categories are important to you and arrange name files accordingly.

Every name is plain! The travel file has made me smile.

When I travel I always have my laptop computer with me. When I get on the plane I open up my name file for the city I will be visiting to review the names of the people I should know when I arrive. As a result, I will not be embarrassed by forgetting someone's name I should know. You will have the same success if you have **a little bit of discipline** to keep good travel files. Remember to be an **ODD** person. That means you should be **O**rganized, **D**isciplined and **D**iligent to be successful.

CHAPTER 14

Name Standards

A complete list of my standards for both first and last names will be made available to you. It would take up a few hundred pages of this book. That is why it is being made available on the web site. The web site address and code to enter the standard names list is located on page 209.

For your own edification and practice you should sit with a phone book in your lap like I did for fifteen to thirty minutes once in a while to make up standards of your own that might not be on my list. Open the book and say names slowly. Many times a picture will be obvious. Other names will require some thought and imagination. It is this very process that I want you to participate in. Experience and application are the only ways for you to become better at anything. You will be amazed at how quickly your ability to picture names will expand if you simply apply yourself to phone book practice and to study my name standards on the web site.

As you practice with a phone book, listen carefully for each syllable. As you develop standards for names and syllables, record them for future review and study. I have already stated that every syllable in a name doesn't have to be used if you develop a standard for it that will work for you. You must be conscious though not to develop standards that will cause confusion with other names. By recording my standards in alphabetical order, it helped me lessen any possible confusion. I suggest that you do the same thing as you work on your standards. The operative words here are **do it**! Watch a little less television and spend some time with a phone book. In other words, be **ODD** about names!

I do want you to know what I use for names that are the same as colors. I develop a standard that automatically reminds me of the color. For the name **Green**, for instance, I use **grass**. **Grass is green**, and I have never met anyone named Grass, so it doesn't cause possible confusion between two names. For the name **Blue**, I use the **sky**. For **Brown** I use **hot fudge**, and for **Black** I use **a black cat**. For the name **White** I can't use snow, because the name Snow is a common name, and I wouldn't know if I saw snow on a person's face whether the name was White or Snow. I use **white paper** for the name **White**. Make sure as you develop your name standards that you don't develop a standard that could cause confusion with another name.

I'll never forget when I was traded to the New York Knicks

basketball team. My new teammates may have heard a little bit about what I did, but I hadn't published any books at the time. I had been too busy as a student and professional basketball player up to that time. On our first trip when we had a particularly long layover in the Chicago O'Hare Airport, I went to a phone booth, opened a phone book and began to study names. After being there for 30 or 40 minutes, I saw Bill Bradley, who later became Senator Bill Bradley from New Jersey, look at me and whisper something into Dave Debusschere's ear. I don't know what he said but perhaps it was, "He has been in that phone booth for over half an hour looking at that phone book and hasn't made a call yet." After another 30 minutes or so, some other new teammates including Willis Reed, Walt Frazier, Earl Monroe, and Phil Jackson, later to be the coach of the Chicago Bulls and Los Angeles Lakers, and my roommate, were all pointing and whispering about this new teammate who seemed to be a phone book freak.

They began to learn about my abilities and habits and began to take advantage of them. Several of my teammates liked to play cards and gamble for small amounts of money during airplane flights to help pass time. They began to lay their bets in the aisles. Red Holtzman, our coach, didn't like the appearance of what was happening, so he put a stop to it. They wanted to continue to play, so they asked for my help. They weren't playing for huge sums but all of the pots contained quite a few dollars. They asked me to keep track of all the bets in my head. When the trip ended, one of the players would ask, "Okay, Jerry, who owes who money and how much?" I would tell them, and they always paid up with no questions asked. They learned to have confidence in my systems and ability.

They had particular confidence in me, because I had memorized every play of every team in the NBA. I knew every play of every one of our opponents by name or number when they called it out. Before almost every game, Red Holtzman would ask, "Okay, Lucas, what plays are they most likely to run tonight?"

We had more plays than any other team in the NBA. Every time an opponent called out a play I simply called out one of our plays that was exactly like it, so we knew what kind of play was going to be run. Was it helpful? You make that decision. The only time I didn't know what was going to be run was when an opponent came out of a time out. Even in those situations, I still had a good idea of what play they might run from experience. The Boston Celtics, for instance, always seemed to run a play they called Ohio when coming out of a time out. I knew its name, because it was the same play they called Ohio during the game. It must have been a play put in by John Havlicek, my roommate at Ohio State. It was a play where a couple of picks were set for John or some other player along the base line to try to open them up for a jump shot. I've used my systems for almost everything through the years, but the use that most people want to learn it for is names and faces.

CHAPTER 15

More Practice

Just as with the eight practice faces used earlier you will see the name spelled out, I will give you a phonetic pronunciation if one is needed. The people you are about to meet are also some of the many people I met on a television talk show. They also are actual people that I described to an artist, so he could recreate them for my teaching sequences.

The first person's name is **Gordon**. The sound-alike word to picture this name is fairly obvious. I simply see a **garden** to picture this name. A **garden** is my standard for **Gordon**. Step number one (1) is completed, because we have listened to, understood and pictured the name.

Next we must look at the face and **select an outstanding facial feature**, which is what **step number two** (2) instructs us to do. Miss **Gordon**'s face is pictured below. Look at it and select what you believe to be the outstanding facial feature. Look for something where you may be able to grow a garden.

I think you might agree with me about the outstanding facial feature. The **large mouth** stood out to me. Step number two (2) is completed.

Step number three (3) instructs us to **connect the pictured name to the outstanding facial feature**. Of course, we developed a picture for this name in step one (1). In this case, it is logical to think of the lar**ge mouth** as being a place to plant a **garden**. Look at the picture of Miss **Gordon**'s face and imagine that a garden is growing out of her mouth. **See the garden growing from seeds to**

mature plants. Imagine that you picked some vegetables out of her mouth as they matured. With such a large garden you will be able to eat for a long time. Make sure to look back at her face and see the picture clearly, and you will see her name on her face. A **garden** will remind you of **Gordon**.

The next person I want you to meet is named **Berger**. The sound-alike word to picture this name is obvious. I simply see a **burger** to picture this name. A **burger** is my standard for **Berger**. Step number one (1) is completed.

Next we must look at the face and **select an outstanding facial feature**, which is what **step number two (2)** instructs us to do. Here is Mr. Berger's face. Look at it and select what you believe to be the outstanding facial feature.

I think his **bald head** is the outstanding facial feature. No doubt, you agreed with me. Step number two (2) is completed.

Step number three (3) instructs us to **connect the pictured name to the outstanding facial feature**. We decided to use a **burger** to picture this name, so we need to **connect a burger to his bald head** in some unique way. Remember to not just casually place the picture for the name on the facial feature. You need to get as much action as possible tied into your facial pictures. Look at Mr. Berger's face and **imagine that a large burger is frying on his bald head**. Imagine that the burger is sizzling and grease is running off of his bald head. Look back at his face and see this happening very clearly. Make sure to see the action.

The next person I want you to meet is named **Tiefenbach** pronounced **tie-fin-back**. The sound-alike word to picture this name is fairly obvious. We will **tie** a fish **fin back** onto something. Step number one (1) is complete. Look at the picture below. It pictures this zip name without a problem.

Next we must look at the face and **select an outstanding facial feature**, which is what **step number two (2)** instructs us to do. Here is Mr. **Tiefenbach**'s face. Look at it and select what you believe to be the outstanding facial feature.

I chose his **full sideburns.** Perhaps you did too. **Step number three (3)** instructs us to **connect the pictured name to the outstanding facial feature**. We decided to **tie** a **fin back** to something to picture this name, so we need to do that in some unique way on his face. Imagine that you used a rope to **tie** his sideburns to a fish **fin back** behind his head. Look back at his face and see this happening very clearly. Make sure to see the action that ties the sideburns to a fish fin in the back of his head, and you will easily see his name on his outstanding facial feature.

The next person I want you to meet is named **Flood**. The sound-alike word that I use for this name is obvious. I use a **flood**. There is no need to make up something else. The name is already tangible. Step number one (1) is complete.

Next we must look at the face and **select an outstanding facial feature**, which is what **step number two (2)** instructs us to do. Mrs. Flood's face is pictured below. Look at it and select what you believe to be the outstanding facial feature.

I think we can easily agree to use her **squinty eyes**. **Step number three (3)** instructs us to **connect the pictured name to the outstanding facial feature**. We need to **connect a flood to her**

squinty eyes in some unique way. Let's imagine that Mrs. **Flood** blinks her eyes rapidly, and a **flood** pours out of them. She continues to blink and raging floodwaters fill the room. The more ridiculous the action is, the easier the pictured name will be to remember. Look back at her face and see that event happening very clearly and you will easily know later that her name is **Flood**.

I am going to give you a quick review before continuing. Do not look back at any of the pictures of the faces during this review. You met a lady with a very large mouth. Think of the face and the picture on the face. Do you know her name? I think you do! You met a man with a totally bald head. Do you know his name? You met a man with very large, full sideburns. Do you know his name? How could you possibly forget it? You also met a lady with very squinty eyes. Do you remember her name? You did real well, didn't you? You should continue to feel good about yourself.

The next person I want you to meet is named **Corcoran** pronounced **core-co-run**. The standard sound-alike word for this name is **cork run**. Step number one (1) is completed.

Next we must look at the face and **select an outstanding facial feature**, which is what **step number two (2)** instructs us to do. Mr. Corcoran is pictured on the next page. Look at his face and select what you believe to be the outstanding facial feature. It is quite obvious.

I used his **goatee**. I'm sure you chose the same feature. Step number two (2) is completed.

Step number three (3) instructs us to **connect the pictured name to the outstanding facial feature**. We decided to use a **cork run**ning to picture his name, so we need to **connect a cork run**ning **to his goatee** in some unique way. Imagine that his goatee is a **cork** that pops itself off of his chin and **run**s all around his face before popping itself back onto his chin. Look back at his face and see that action happening very clearly. See the **cork** popping, **run**ning and popping back on to his chin.

The next person I want you to meet is named **Bacon**. The sound-alike word for this name is obvious. Once again, the name is already tangible. We will simply see **bacon**. Step number one

(1) is completed.

The **next step** involves looking at the face to **select an outstanding facial feature**. Mr. Bacon's face is pictured below. Look at his face and select what you believe to be the outstanding facial feature.

I think we could agree very quickly on his **big, broad nose**. **Step number three (3)** instructs us to **connect the pictured name to the outstanding facial feature**. We need to connect **bacon** to his **big, broad nose** in some unique way. I look for anything to make it easy for me to remember the person's name. In this case, I imagined that his **nose** was an oven, and I was **bakin' bacon** in the big, broad nose shaped oven. I actually used two words, bakin' and bacon, to picture the name on the face. Look back at his face and see that picture very clearly before continuing.

The next person I want you to meet is named **Diratsos** pronounced **di-rat-soas**. Say these two syllables a few times and think of a possible sound-alike word to picture this name. I use a **de**ad **rat sews** for this name. It isn't the exact sound, but it is close enough to work, and it is a vivid picture. In this case I only use the first two letters of "dead" toward the picture of the name. It doesn't cause me a problem, because it is my standard for this name, and I know not to pronounce the "ad" in the word "dead."

The **next step** involves looking at the face to **select an outstanding facial feature**. You see a picture of Mr. **Diratsos**'s face below. Look at it and select what you believe to be the outstanding facial feature.

I think we could agree very on his **cleft chin**. **Step number three (3)** instructs us to **connect the pictured name to the outstanding facial feature**. We decided to use **de**ad **rat sews** to picture his name, so we need to connect a **de**ad **rat** that **sews** to his **cleft chin** in some unique way. What I used should be fairly obvious. I imagined that a dead rat was sewn into the cleft chin. Someone sews and sews until the dead rat disappears into the cleft chin. Look back at his face and see that event happening very clearly. It isn't a very delightful thought, but it is very memorable.

The next person I want you to meet is named **Maddox**, and I use a **mad ox** to picture this name. Step number one (1) is completed.

The **next step** involves looking at the face to **select an outstanding facial**. Miss Maddox's face is pictured below. This will be the last face to be learned in this practice drill. Look at it and

select what you believe to be the outstanding facial feature.

I think we could agree on her **turned up nose. Step number three (3)** instructs us to **connect the pictured name to the outstanding facial feature**. We decided to use a **mad ox** to picture her name, so we need to connect a **mad ox** to her **turned up nose** in some unique way. The picture is fairly obvious once again. Imagine that a very **mad ox** charged into her **nose** quite violently and **turned** it **up**. Look back at her face and see that event happening very clearly. Imagine that the ox stands back and snorts after turning up the nose to admire its work.

Now it's time for a test to see if you remember the names of these eight people. I will show you a picture of their faces again. When you see each face, do the following:

1) Look at the face carefully and recall the outstanding facial feature that was selected.

2) See the action picture that we connected to the facial feature.

3) Translate the sound-alike word for the name back to the actual name to recall the name.

CHAPTER 16

More about First Names

I have only discussed first names to this point when I discussed the long-term name retrieval cards and used Bill Berg as an example. You will recall that I added his first name to the facial action picture to complete the story for his first and last names. A quick review reminds us that Bill **Berg** had a long scar on his left cheek. We imagined that he fell on an ice**berg** and cut his cheek. This attached his last name to his outstanding facial feature. We then imagined that he reached into his pocket, pulled out a dollar **bill** and slapped it on the cut to stop the bleeding. This attached his first name to his outstanding facial feature along with his last name. All of this information was recorded on his long-term name retrieval file card for later review. In the review process the first name could easily be recalled along with the last name.

This is the same process that should be applied for all first names. You will recall that I suggested that you always have a pen and paper with you, so you can record the names of people as you meet them. As a result, these names can be reviewed during the function where the meeting occurred, and you can record them on retrieval cards. As always **a little bit of discipline** is required for you to be successful.

A list of literally hundreds of first names with my suggestions for sound-alike standards appears on the Doctor Memory™ web site for your review or downloading. Remember that the address and special entry code for the names and faces aids are on page 209. Familiarize yourself with as many standards for first names as possible. The more you know the more success you will enjoy.

Whether we use a first or last name at a particular function obviously depends on the circumstance. A formal gathering will require the use of last names, but first names are used more times than not, and first names are being discussed at this time. I recently returned from a three-day event on the big island of Hawaii where I taught for Active Software. There were a total of eighty people at this function, and I had never met any of them. I met four of them on the bus to the hotel, and they introduced themselves with first names only. As is my habit I listened very attentively with my elephant ears, locked in these first names and used them in my conversation on the way to the hotel. The first names were Jim, Mike, Ted and Becky. It was obvious to me that Ted and Becky were traveling together, so they probably were husband and wife, since they were seated together. It was also obvious to me that first names, and not last names, were going to be preferred for this particular function.

When I arrived at the hotel I asked for a list of all the people who would be attending the three-day function. They were listed as either an attendee or a guest of an attendee. The attendees were on the left of the page, and the guests were on the right of the page directly across from the name of the attendee. I first looked for the names of Ted and Becky as I scanned the list. I found them very quickly and found that they were married and their last name was Liu, which is pronounced Loo. I marked them on the list and mentally recalled their faces as a quick review. I next looked for the name Jim. I found two listings for Jim as well as a James. I couldn't zero in on the last name of this person just yet, but I had him narrowed down to one of three last names. Next I looked for the name Mike. There was only one Mike, but the name Michael was listed twice. Once again, I couldn't zero in on the last name of this person just yet, but I had him narrowed down to one of three last names as well. My plan of success was already in progress.

I met Kerry Anne McArdle who was coordinating the meeting and asked her specific questions about the people I had met on the bus. When I described Jim I found out that he was Jim Green, the CEO of Active Software. He was easy to describe because he had a beard. When I described Mike I found out that his last name was Hughes. He was also easy to describe because of his closely cropped hair. I went to my list and marked Jim and Mike off. I know knew their first and last names. My narrowing down process had begun.

Jim invited me to his room to watch the final game of the Final Four, which eventually was won by Michigan State. I had played in three final games of the Final Four myself while attending Ohio State University. It was obvious to me that Jim had invited several people to watch the game, since many chairs were set up facing the television. I was the first person who arrived at his room and would be able to meet people as they arrived. As always, I was very attentive as each person announced his or her names to me. Very quickly I discovered the name of another Mike. His name was Mike Ping. Since I enjoy playing golf that was a particular easy name to picture.

By the way, my golf was what caused me to be contracted to speak for Active Software in the first place. I play on the CPT, which is the Celebrity Players' Tour. John Brodie, the great San Francisco Forty Niner quarterback, is also a member of our tour. John knew about my memory and learning abilities, because I normally demonstrate my ability to remember names by remembering the names of more than a hundred people at our extravaganza banquet at each tour stop. I meet our pro-am players as they are eating at the banquet, then go to the stage and call out all of their names during the entertainment phase of the banquet. John's daughter Cammie is Jim Green's personal assistant, and she called John to ask him who from our tour might be a good presenter at their sales rewards function. John recommended me, and Cammie called me to make the arrangements. I talked to her several times on the phone but had never met her.

I need to get back to Jim Green's Final Four party. Cammie Brodie was one of the first to arrive at the party, so I got to put a name with a face. I met Jim Diamond and narrowed down the list of Jim names. As people continued to arrive I was very attentive to listening and doing **my thing**. When the room began to fill up some of the people walked past me and there was no introduction. The game was underway, and people were interested in watching the game more than being introduced. But I still was being attentive. I looked at and reviewed the people in attendance as the game proceeded. My reviews locked the names into my mind more and more securely.

I heard one couple that I didn't meet addressed as Allan and Becky. I say this so you can understand that you can remember and register names when no introduction takes place if you are just listening carefully to conversation. When I went back to the room and looked at my list I discovered that Allan and Becky's last name was Hogue. By having a little bit of discipline I was having success and would be able to call all of those people by name the next time I saw them during the three day function.

Mike Ping asked me to have some fun with the Looney brothers. They did not attend the game in Jim's room. He told me that Tom Looney had played college basketball and that he wanted me to tell Tom that I heard that his brother Bill was a much better basketball player than he was. Once again I was becoming more familiar with names before even meeting the people. When I met Tom at the evening party I made mention of what Mike had asked me to say. He laughed loudly and it opened up an opportunity for a friendship that continued with the Looney brothers and Jim Diamond on the golf course the next day.

Each time I went back to my room I took the time to mark off and review all the people I had met. As the list grew, so did my knowledge of their names and faces because of my continuing review process. I only invested a little bit of time in the review process, but I was rewarded with the ability of knowing the first names of all of the people I had met. I also knew their last names, but this was a first name function.

Hopefully you have learned something from my Active Software experience that will help you. Always be attentive and listen even if you aren't involved in a particular conversation. You will learn names of people you don't even meet if you are alert and have **a little bit of discipline**.

In this instance my name retrieval file system was given to me in the list of attendees and their guests. I had their first and last names, and all I had to do was match the face to the names that I had familiarized myself with in my room. When I have such a list I go over it several times to familiarize myself with the names before I even meet the people. At least I will be more comfortable with the names and won't have any surprises thrown at me. Normally I would have asked for the list prior to the meeting, but I was so busy doing the final edit on Dr. Memory's™ *Picture Perfect Spanish* book that I let it slide. My **little bit of discipline** slid away from me in this instance, but I made up for it when I arrived in Hawaii. Try not to let this happen to you. It seldom happens to me, because I know it can mean the difference between success and failure.

CHAPTER 17

Feature Faces

On the next page you see a picture of Whozit™ the elephant preparing to enter a double, double feature length movie. He is excited because he is going to learn more about faces and their features. He will be able to double his ability. You will too as you study Dr. Memory's™ Feature Faces that are soon to appear at a movie house near you.

I have created almost a hundred faces for your practice purposes. I call them **Feature Faces**. They have a two-fold purpose. They will help you realize that there are many facial features that can be used, and you can practice remembering names by attaching the names I have given them to their faces. The names, facial features and sound-alikes for the names will be listed first, so they will not be near the face. You should look back and forth from the name to the face during this practice process. Only a last name has been given to the first six faces. You can make up first names for these people at a later time. My suggestion is that you attach the last names first and then attach the made-up first names at a later time. Make sure you see each picture on each face very clearly before going to the next face. I have given picture suggestions for the first and last names of all of the faces past the first six. You will learn many more standards for names as you go through this practice drill. When you learn standards for names you will know how to picture those particular names forever, and your skill will raise to another level, perhaps even double as Whozit's™ did.

Look back and forth from the name to the face and see my suggested picture on the face vividly with as much action as possible. Review each face again after you learn every new name and face. This review process is vital for your success. Making it a part of your routine will lead to success. After doing this for six or eight faces look back at the faces and try to recall the names that go with the faces. Continue this process from time to time until you have learned all of the names. You certainly don't have to learn all of the names in one sitting. Study them at your leisure but make sure to finish this **Feature Faces** drill. It will increase your ability, knowledge and confidence. You may want to assign names of your own choosing to many of these faces without using my suggestions for even more practice. The faces are pictured beginning on page 192. Have fun with these faces.

Face # 1 – Mr. Rapp – Long Nose

Sound-Alike – Wrap

Picture – See yourself **wrap**ping a big bandage around his nose. Then imagine the **wrap** hanging down from his nose. See this imaginary action happening very clearly in your mind.

You will find Mr. Rapp's face pictured on page 192. Keep your finger at that page as you look back and forth from the name and the facial picture I have suggested to the face. I have separated the names and faces, so you wouldn't be tempted to look at the name during the review process.

Face # 2 – Miss Trapp – Sunken Cheeks

Sound-Alike – An animal trap

Picture – Imagine that her cheeks are sunken because a hunter placed **trap**s in them. See the **trap**s snapping shut and causing her cheeks to be even more sunken.

Face # 3 – Mr. Smith – Bushy Eyebrows

Sound-Alike – A blacksmith hammer

Picture – See yourself using a black**smith** hammer to beat his eyebrows into the shape of a horseshoe.

Face # 4 – Mr. Barber – Bags Under Eyes

Sound-Alike – A barber

Picture – Imagine that a **barber** uses his scissors to trim the bags under his eyes. See pieces of the bags dropping as the **barber** snips away.

Face # 5 – Mr. Portillo (pour tea yo) – Long Moustache

Sound-Alike – Pour tea – **Pour tea** is my standard for **Portillo**. Even though the last syllable of the name isn't included in the standard it doesn't cause me a problem. I know to add the "yo" sound to my standard sound. As I told you earlier, I sometimes use only a couple of syllable as a standard for a four or five syllable name. If I know what the standard represents it doesn't cause any confusion.

Picture – See yourself using a large teapot to **pour tea** all over his moustache. See the **pour**ed **tea** dripping off of the moustache.

Face # 6 – Mr. Bellamy – Parted Hair
Sound-Alike – Bell me or a bell with measles
Picture – Imagine he is saying, "My hair is parted because some-one threw a **bell** at **me**." See yourself throwing a **bell** with **me**asles at him.

Review these six faces again at this point. During the review process if you happen to forget a name simply go back and look at the name and the face another time to lock the facial picture in more securely.

Face # 7 – Skip Crouse – Round Jaw
Sound-Alikes – Skip rope and a grouse (the bird)
Picture – His round jaw looks like a **skip** rope. A **grouse** jerks the rope off of his face and uses it to skip rope around his round jaw.

Face # 8 – Mike Webster – Crossed Eyes
Sound-Alikes – A microphone (a mike) and web stir (stirring spi-der webs)
Picture – A microphone, a **mike**, is between his eyes, and he is watching a spider spin a web around it. That is why his eyes are crossed. Imagine that the spider takes the **web** and **stir**s it into his eyes. The spider then pulls on the web to try to uncross his eyes.

Face # 9 – Carol Nusbaum – Big Lips

Sound-Alikes – Christmas carol and a newspaper bomb

Picture – She is using her big lips to sing a Christmas **carol**. A newspaper boy doesn't like her singing, so he wraps a newspaper around a bomb and sticks it into her mouth. The **news bomb** explodes and her lips get even bigger. This is really big news.

Face # 10 – Phyllis Winters – Afro Hairdo

Sound-Alikes – Fill us up and winter weather

Picture – Imagine that a winter wind with blowing snow is **fill**ing her hair (**us**) up with snow. Imagines when the **winter** fill up (us) is completed that her Afro hairdo turns white.

Face # 11 – Sandi Bevilaqua – Long Eyelashes

Sound-Alikes – Sandy and devil aqua (aqua means "water" in Spanish)

Picture – Imagine that she blinks her long eyelashes and sand flies out of them to make everything **sandy**. They are still full of sand, so the **devil** pours his Spanish water "**aqua**" on her eyelashes to wash the sand away.

Face # 12 – Clark Smith – Big Nose

Sound-Alikes – A Clark candy bar or Clark Kent and a blacksmith hammer

Picture – We already used the last name Smith for face number three, but you will find that you will not get confused. Each face has its particular feature to use, and the review process eliminates confusion. Imagine that his nose is so big that **Clark** Kent used a black**smith** hammer to beat on it in order to make it smaller. You could see a **Clark** candy bar being used as a black**smith** hammer to reshape his nose. Choose which picture you believe will work better for you and see it happening very clearly on his face.

Review faces 7 through 12 again at this point. During the review process if you happen to forget a name simply go back and look at the name and the face another time to lock the facial picture in more securely. Now review faces 1 through 12. Continued review locks the names into your mind more and more securely. This review process takes very little time, and is a vital part of being successful. As you apply this process during this Feature Faces drill you will be developing good practice habits that will spill over into the actual introductory process with real people. Practice makes perfect.

Face # 13 – Anne Bainbridge – Long Full Bangs
Sound-Alikes – An ant and pain bridge
Picture – Imagine that a colony of **an**ts are trying to walk across her bangs. There is so much hair that it is a real **pain** for the ants, so they build a **bridge** to cross her bangs. See the busy little ants doing their thing on her face very clearly before continuing.

Face # 14 – Judd Arnold – Scar on Neck

Sound-Alikes – A judge and an iron that is old

Picture – Imagine this man is in a courtroom and is mouthing off to the **jud**ge. The judge got fed up with him and threw an old iron (**iron old**) at him and scarred his throat with the tip of the iron. I guess the judge impressed his point on Mr. Judd Arnold.

Face # 15 – Bud Hyde – Cleft Chin

Sound-Alikes – A flower bud and hide something

Picture – Imagine that you **hide** a flower **bud** in his cleft chin and forget about it. Then imagine that other flower **bud**s start to pop out of his cleft chin and **hide** themselves back in the cleft chin.

Face # 16 – Pearl Hurwitz – Thin Lips

Sound-Alikes – A string of pearls and her wits (brains)

Picture – Imagine she has a thin string of **pearl**s for lips. Then see her beginning to spit the pearls up one at a time. The pearls enter her brain, **her wits**, and collect there.

Just the thought of making up these pictures causes you to be much more aware of the names. Even if the pictures didn't work you would be much more aware of the names because your mind is concentrating on the job at hand and isn't absent doing something else. But the pictures do work, and the whole process locks the names securely into your mind.

Face # 17 – Hank Weber – Turned up Nose

Sound-Alikes – A hanky and a spider (a webber)

Picture – Imagine that a spider, a **webber**, attaches a web to his nose and pulls it up on top of his head. That is why he has a turned up nose. Then imagine that this tickles Hank and he takes out a **hanky** to blow his nose.

Face # 18 – Homer Fontaine – Low Full Cheeks

Sound-Alikes – A "homer" in baseball and a fountain – Even though a fountain doesn't sound exactly like the name Fontaine, I have no problem. A fountain is my standard for Fontaine, and I know to say Fontaine and not fountain. For the actual name "Fountain" I see a different kind of fountain in my mind. As a result, I don't confuse the names Fontaine and Fountain. You can do the same thing for other similar names, so you won't confuse them as well.

Picture – Imagine that he was in the stands at a baseball game. Two **homer**s were hit and landed inside his mouth. That is why his cheeks are full. The balls hurt his mouth. So he spit them into a large **fountain** at the ballpark.

Review faces 13 through 18 again at this point. During the review process if you happen to forget a name simply go back and look at the name and the face another time to lock the facial picture in more securely. Now review faces 1 through 18.

Face # 19 – Kerry Zhukov – No Chin
Sound-Alikes – Carry something and zoo cough or zoo coffin
Picture – Imagine she lost her chin in a zoo. Perhaps one of the zoo animals jerked it off of her face. Then imagine that the animal carried (**carry**) her chin to a **zoo coff**in and placed it there. May her chin rest in peace.

Face # 20 – David Greenbaum – Thin Moustache
Sound-Alikes – A sling is my standard for David. David used a sling in the Bible to slay Goliath. A green bomb is my picture for Greenbaum.
Picture – Imagine that you knock the thin moustache off of his face with a sling (**David**). Then imagine that you use the sling to toss a **green** grass **bomb** at his upper lip. The bomb explodes, and he now has a thin, green, grass moustache.

Face # 21 – Bob Lacey – Round Face
Sound-Alikes – A fishing bobber or bobbing for apples and shoelaces or lacing something up
Picture – Imagine his face is round like a fishing **bob**ber. See it bobbing up and down. Imagine that you use shoelaces to **lace** up (**lacey** up) his eyes, ears nose and mouth; so water can't seep into your bobber and sink it.

Face # 22 – Fred Logan – Full Beard
Sound-Alikes – Afraid and low gun

Picture – Imagine all of a sudden his beard stands straight up, because he is **afraid** of something. He is afraid because a thief stuck a gun in the low part of his beard (**low gun**). See this picture clearly before continuing.

Face # 23 – Cliff Green – Hump Nose

Sound-Alikes – A cliff and grass (it is green)

Picture – Imagine his nose is a big **cliff** with a hump of rock on it. See **green**, slick grass growing on the rock. Imagine that kids are sliding down the slick, **green** grass on the **cliff**. Even though you used grass earlier for Mr. Greenbaum, you will not get confused. The review process eliminates any confusion. You will see for yourself when you participate in your review. I ask you to do all of these drills, so your fears and doubts will be eliminated.

Face # 24 – Ruby Weaver – Sunken Eyes

Sound-Alikes – A ruby (the gem) or a rude bee and a weaver of cloth

Picture – Imagine her eyes are sunken because a **ru**de **bee** threw a **ruby** at each eye. Both sound-alikes for Ruby were used to impress the first name on your mind more securely. Imagine that a **weaver** took the rubies out of her eyes and weaved them into a mask to hide her sunken eyes.

Review faces 19 through 24 again at this point. During the review process if you happen to forget a name simply go back and look at the name and the face another time to lock the facial picture in more securely. Now review faces 1 through 24.

Face # 25 – Paul Andrews – Slick Hair
Sound-Alikes – A pole and an ant or an aunt that drew pictures
Picture – Imagine a **pole** is stuck in his slick hair. The lotion holds it securely. Then imagine an **ant** slid down the pole and **drew** a picture in his slick, wet hair.

Face # 26 – Stella Finley – Squinty Eyes
Sound-Alikes – Stale and fin lay (lay a fish fin)
Picture – Imagine her eyes are squinting because **stale** fish **fin**s are **lay**ing on her eye lids. Excuse the bad grammar. As she blinks her eyes imagine that **stale** fish **fin**s fly out and **lay** all over her face.

Face # 27 – Olive Kennedy – Long Thin Neck
Sound-Alikes – An olive and a can of "D" cell batteries or a can with letter "D's" on it
Picture – Imagine her neck is a long, thin **can** full **of** "D" cell batteries. Then imagine an **olive** runs up and down the outside of the can. What an electrically charged neck!

Face # 28 – Marion Carter – Big Lower Lip
Sound-Alikes – Marryin' and a garter or a car with tar
Picture – Imagine he is in the middle of his wedding ceremony. The pastor is **marryin'** him. Imagine his bride's **garter** breaks and

snaps his lip. That is why it is swollen and big.

Face # 29 – Grace Bingham – Tall Forehead
Sound-Alikes – Saying grace or a "G" on a race car and a bingo ham or a big ham
Picture – Imagine "**G**" **race** cars are racing on her forehead. The winner of the race is going to win a **big ham**.

Face # 30 – Buck O'Toole – Bald Head – Little Hair
Sound-Alikes – A buck deer or a buck (money) and an old tool
Picture – Imagine a **buck** deer used its antlers to scrape most of his hair off, so it could eat it. It must have been a tough winter. Then imagine that Mr. O'Toole uses an **old tool** to try to pull the rest of his hair up to the top of his head.

Review faces 25 through 30 again at this point. During the review process if you happen to forget a name simply go back and look at the name and the face another time to lock the facial picture in more securely. Now review faces 1 through 30.

Face # 31 – Frank Rakowski – Big Jaw
Sound-Alikes – A frank (a hot dog) and red cow ski
Picture – Imagine he wrapped a foot long **frank** (hot dog) around his big jaw, so a **red cow** could **ski** down the slick frank. See this action very clearly. See the red frank and the red cow skiing very clearly on this face.

Face # 32 – Ben Walcott - Hairlip
Sound-Alikes – To bend something and a wall cot
Picture – Imagine he ran into a wall and put a **ben**d in his lip. He bounced off of the **wall** and landed in an army **cot.**

Face # 33 – Kelly Oliphant – Eyebrows Together
Sound-Alike – Kelp and elephant – Kelp is a form of seaweed that grows in the ocean.
Picture – Imagine his eyebrows are made of **kel**p. They have become so entangled that he had to hire an **elephant** to pull them apart.

Face # 34 – Bridget Tucker – Long Chin
Sound-Alikes – Bridge it and tuck her
Picture – Imagine her chin is so long that it could be used to **bridge** something (**it**). After the bridge was stretched out, it is **tuck**ed into a place far away from h**er.** The bridge becomes a **tucker.**

Face # 35 – Ester Coyle – Wide Nose
Sound-Alike – To stir and a coil (a coil of wire or a coiled spring)
Picture – Imagine she places a **coil**ed spring around her nose and begins to **stir** it to try to make her nose smaller. Remember that **stir** is my standard for **Ester,** and every time something is being **stir**red, I know the name is **Ester.**

Face # 36 – Eugene Thomas – Bushy Sideburns

Sound-Alikes – "U" jeans and a tom-tom with a map of the US on it (the USA) – For "U" jeans I imagine U-shaped or horseshoe shaped branded jeans.

Picture – Imagine he placed "**U**" **jean**s on the side of his head for sideburns. See the horseshoes falling off of the jeans. Imagine that they bounce on **tom**-toms with a map of the **US** on them. Just seeing tom-toms without the map works for me, because I use a tom-tom as my standard for the last name Thomas.

Review faces 31 through 36 again at this point. During the review process if you happen to forget a name simply go back and look at the name and the face another time to lock the facial picture in more securely. Now review faces 1 through 36.

Face # 37 – Madge Dahlquist – Full Round Cheeks

Sound-Alikes – Magic and doll twist – Since "doll twist" is my standard for Dahlquist, I don't call the person Miss Dolltwist. I know my standards and how to interpret them. So will you if you have **a little bit of discipline**.

Picture – Imagine she placed a **doll** doing the **twist** into her mouth. That is why her cheeks are so full. See the doll twisting around. Since she is a magician she taps her cheeks with a **mag**ic wand, and the doll disappears just like **mag**ic.

Face # 38 – Leo Graff – Cauliflower Ears

Sound-Alikes – Leo the lion and a graph

Picture – Imagine his ears are cauliflowered because he wrestled **Leo** the lion for years in the circus. Then imagine that Leo scratched a **graph** onto his big ears.

Face # 39 – Clyde Bloomquist - Goatee

Sound-Alikes – To glide and bloom twist – I always use twist for the "quist" sound.

Picture – Imagine a flower begins to **bloom** in his goatee. Then imagine that he **twist**s it off and it **glide**s down his body. See that same action happening again and again.

Face # 40 – Priscilla Rector – Slanted Eyebrows

Sound-Alikes – Press silly and wreck tar or wreck tore

Picture – Imagine she uses an iron and **press**es her eyebrows. What a **silly** thing to do. As she presses them they **wreck** together, and you reached out and **tore** them off of her face. This may not be the most logical picture in the world, but just thinking of it and seeing it will cause it to work. Observation will take place, and the information will register on your mind.

Face # 41 – Maggi Mendoza – Big Eyes

Sound-Alikes – A magnet or maggot and men doze

Picture – Imagine her eyes are big **mag**nets. They are so powerful that they pull a couple of **men** who were **doz**ing into them. Those

men won't **doze** for long. She has very magnetic, attractive eyes.

Face # 42 – Grant Gallagher – Thick Neck

Sound-Alikes – Granite rock and a gal saying "grr"

Picture – Imagine his neck is so thick and strong looking because it is made of **gran**ite rock. A **gal** taps his granite neck and says, "**Grr**," that feels like grrranite.

Review faces 37 through 42 again at this point. During the review process if you happen to forget a name simply go back and look at the name and the face another time to lock the facial picture in more securely. Now review faces 1 through 42.

Face # 43 – Curtis Glick – Vertical Lines Around Mouth

Sound-Alikes – A curtain made of tissue and to click something

Picture – Imagine the long lines are electrically operated **cur**tains made of **tis**sue. Imagine you **click** a switch and the curtains open and shut again and again.

Face # 44 – Guy Reineche – Thick Glasses - You will recall that I said not to use glasses unless you were sure the person couldn't see without them. There is no doubt he will be wearing his glasses every place he goes.

Sound-Alikes – A guide and rain a key

Picture – Imagine it begins to **rain a key**, then another and another. Also imagine that the small key raindrops adhere to his glasses so thickly that he needs a **gui**de to lead him around. He probably does anyway because he can't see very well.

Face # 45 – Zelda Waite – Beauty Mark
Sound-Alikes – Sail a dud or sell a dud and a weight
Picture – Imagine a **sail**or who is a **du**d sails his boat into her beauty mark and knocks it off. The **sail**or says, "**Duh**." When it falls off she places it on a scale to determine its **weight**.

Face # 46 – Barry Powell – Egg-shaped Head
Sound-Alikes – A berry and powerful oil
Picture – Imagine the shape of his head reminds you of a big **berry**. Since you want to bake a berry pie, you use a **pow**erful hose to squirt **oil** on his head, so you can slip the big berry away.

Face # 47 – Forrest Neuhause – Flattop Haircut
Sound-Alikes – A forest and a new house
Picture – Imagine a **forest** had been growing out of his head. Lumberjacks leveled it off. Also imagine that the lumber was used to build a **new house** on the flat spot on top of his head.

Face # 48 – Neal Dutton – Wrinkled Neck
Sound-Alikes – To kneel and a button
Picture – Imagine someone **kneel**s down on the wrinkles on his neck and pulls **button**s out of the wrinkles.

Review faces 43 through 48 again at this point. During the review process if you happen to forget a name simply go back and look at the name and the face another time to lock the facial picture in more securely. Now review faces 1 through 48.

Face # 49 – Hale Cottle – Crooked Mouth

Sound-Alikes – Hail and cot oil

Picture – Imagine his mouth was knocked crooked by falling **hail**. Then imagine that he spit some hail out of his mouth onto an army **cot** covered with **oil**. The hail won't stay on the cot because of the slick oil.

Face # 50 – Barb Upshaw – Wavy Hair

Sound-Alikes – Barbed wire and up shawl

Picture – Imagine the waves in her hair are actually wavy **barb**ed wire. Then imagine that you throw a shawl up (**up shaw**l) and it gets stuck on the barbed wire. See the picture clearly.

Face # 51 – Vance Monahan – Big Ears

Sound-Alikes – Vans and a monocle with a handle

Picture – Imagine his big ears are waving down a couple of **vans**. Then see the vans crashing into his ears. A doctor then used a **mon**ocle with **a han**dle on it to examine the trapped vans.

Face # 52 – Billie Lynch – Long Thin Nose

Sound-Alikes – A billy club and to lynch or hang someone – You could also use a linchpin.

Picture – Imagine her nose is a long thin **billy** club. Then imagine that her nose, the billy club, was stretched out even farther because it was **lynch**ed on a hanging tree. See it hanging from the tree in your mind.

Face # 53 – Claire Fraser – Wrinkled Lips
Sound-Alikes – An eclair and a freezer
Picture – Imagine she just ate an **eclair** that she took out of a **freezer**. The cold eclair wrinkled up her lips.

Face # 54 – Stephanie Gerstein – Furrowed Brow
Sound-Alikes – Stuff a knee and curse stein
Picture – Imagine her brow is furrowed because you **stuff**ed **a knee** into her brow. I like to see myself involved in the action picture when possible. Afterwards she **curse**s you and throws a **stein** of beer in your face.

Review faces 49 through 54 again at this point. During the review process if you happen to forget a name simply go back and look at the name and the face another time to lock the facial picture in more securely. Now review faces 1 through 54.

Face # 55 – Flint Spencer – Mole on Nose
Sound-Alikes – A flint stone and spin sir
Picture – Imagine the mole on his nose is a **flint** stone. It starts to

spin and sparks fly from it. You make a request and say, "Could you please stop the **spin**ning, **sir**. The sparks are annoying me."

Face # 56 – Kendall Lipinski – Pencil Thin Moustache
Sound-Alikes – A candle and lip in ski
Picture – Imagine his moustache is actually two pencil thin, taper **candles**. He jerks the waxed moustache candles off and uses them as skis. He isn't a good skier, so he falls down and sticks a ski in his lip (**lip in ski**).

Face # 57 – Larry Klaus – Full Short Beard
Sound-Alikes – A lariat and claws
Picture – Imagine you toss a **lari**at around his beard. He then **claws** at it with his nails to remove it.

Face # 58 – Archibald Endicott – Long Chin
Sound-Alikes – An arch that is bald and the end of a cot
Picture – Imagine his chin is an upside **arch** that **is bald**. It certainly doesn't have any hair. I sometimes use some screwy pictures, but it doesn't matter, because the thought process and picture work no matter how screwy they might be. Now imagine that his big chin is so heavy that it causes him to lose his balance and fall on the **end of** an army **cot**.

Face # 59 – Boyd Kramer – Scar at Left Eye
Sound-Alikes – Buoyed and a creamer

Picture – Imagine he got the scar when he ran into a buoy. He got **buoyed** while water skiing in a huge **creamer** instead of a lake.

Face # 60 – Harley Blazek – Big Ears and Earlobes

Sound-Alikes – A Harley Davidson motorcycle and a blaze in a sack

Picture – Imagine his ears caught on fire from the exhaust of a **Harley**. See yourself jerking his ears off as they blaze. To stop the **bla**ze you stuffed them into a fireproof **sack**.

Review faces 55 through 60 again at this point. During the review process if you happen to forget a name simply go back and look at the name and the face another time to lock the facial picture in more securely. Now review faces 1 through 60.

Face # 61 – Mel Pacheco – Short Beard, No Moustache

Sound-Alikes – Melt and pay check

Picture – Imagine his white beard is made of ice, and it begins to **mel**t. As it melts it drips all over his **pay check**, and he says, "**Oh**." The "oh" sound isn't really necessary, since my standard is a paycheck, but I put it in anyway. If you feel you need a particular sound to be impressed on your mind you can add it.

Face # 62 – Jesse O'Hara – Walrus-like Moustache

Sound-Alikes – Jesse James (the bandit) and old hair

Picture – Imagine **Jesse** James stole his moustache. He was told that gold was stored in it. When he got away and examined it he discovered it was just **old hair** with no valuables attached, so he threw it away.

Face # 63 – Flora Dabney – Beauty Mark at Right Eye
Sound-Alikes – A floor and dab a knee
Picture – Imagine she **dab**s her beauty mark with her **knee**. That is quite a trick. She dabs it so hard that it falls onto the **floor**, and she says, "**Uh**."

Face # 64 – Donald Coyne – Neat Long Sideburns
Sound-Alikes – Donald Duck and a coin
Picture – Imagine **Donald** Duck lifts up his long, neat sideburns and hides **coin**s under them. He might lift them up with his duck-bill to make the picture more vivid.

Face # 65 – Nellie Losh – Wrinkled Face
Sound-Alikes – Nail an eel and slosh
Picture – Imagine the wrinkles are really eels that are **slosh**ing all over her face. To keep them still imagine that you **nail** the **eel**s to her face.

Face # 66 – Alexander Hicks – Dark Circles Under Eyes
Sound-Alikes – Owl legs sander and hicks (hillbillies) or hiccups
Picture – Imagine an **owl** with sandpaper on its **legs** uses its **legs** as **sander**s to try to sand the dark circles away. The man gets **hic**cups

during the sanding, and the owl complains.

Review faces 61 through 66 again at this point. During the review process if you happen to forget a name simply go back and look at the name and the face another time to lock the facial picture in more securely. Now review faces 1 through 66.

Face # 67 – Edith McComb – Short Thin Neck
Sound-Alikes – Eat dust with a lisp (duth) and a mucky comb
Picture – Imagine she wants to gain some weight in her neck, and a friend told her to **eat** some dust (**duth**) for that purpose. She did, and then spit mucky dust out that collects around her neck. She then combs the **muck**y dust away with a large **comb**.

Face # 68 – Herman Oppenheimer – Large Adam's Apple
Sound-Alikes – Her man and open hammer
Picture – Imagine the lady who loves this man always tells others about the cute, large Adam's apple that **her man** has as she strokes it. He thinks it is too big, so he **open**s it up with a **hammer** to take part of it out to make it smaller.

Face # 69 – Edwin Decker – Crow's Feet Lines at Eyes
Sound-Alikes – A head wind and deck her
Picture – Imagine a h**ead win**d blew so hard on his head that it caused the crow's feet lines to appear at his eyes. He found out that the wind came from a large fan that was held by a lady and he

decked **her** by knocking her down on her patio deck.

Face # 70 – Donna Percival – Curved Lines above Eyes

Sound-Alikes – Dawn and a purse that is full

Picture – Imagine the lines are the rays of the sun as it rises at **dawn**. She doesn't like the lines, so she jerked them off and stuffed them into her **purse** that **is** already **full**.

Face # 71 – Conrad Kobus – Small Nose

Sound-Alikes – A convict rat and a cold bus

Picture – Imagine a **con**vict **rat** stole the other part of his nose and left the small portion you can see. The rat jumped into a **cold bus** to make his getaway. What a rat to nose into other people's business.

Face # 72 – Sarah Feliciano – Wide Mouth

Sound-Alikes – The Sahara desert and fleas in a piano

Picture – Imagine her mouth is as wide and as dry as the **Sahara** desert. She coughed and spit sand from the desert all over **fleas** in a **piano**. That is unusual mouth music.

Review faces 67 through 72 again at this point. During the review process if you happen to forget a name simply go back and look at the name and the face another time to lock the facial picture in more securely. Now review faces 1 through 72.

Face # 73 – John Humphries – Pointed Ears

Sound-Alikes – A john (a toilet) and hump freeze

Picture – Imagine his ears remind you of the flush handle of a **john**, a toilet. See yourself pulling down on his ear to flush the john, and freon runs out of his ear and forms a **hump** that **freeze**s on his ear. I guess freon will freeze about anything.

Face # 74 – Duane Murdock – Sleepy Eyelids

Sound-Alikes – A drain (If spoken like Daffy Duck it would be a dwain.) and a myrrh dock (myrrh is a perfume)

Picture – Imagine something is draining, **dwain**ing, out of his eyes. He shut them, because he wants the draining to stop. **Myrrh** and not water is draining from his eyes. The myrrh is draining onto a **dock**.

Face # 75 – Bailey Bernard – Sideburns and Moustache Grow Together

Sound-Alikes – A bale of something or to bail water or to pay bail and burn hard

Picture – Imagine that he wanted to get rid of his sideburns and moustache, so he set them on fire. They wouldn't **burn** because they had become so **hard** over time. So, he called a farmer friend and asked him to cut and **bail** his moustache and beard. See the farmer doing his work.

Face # 76 – Calvert Galbreath – Moustache and Goatee

Sound-Alikes – A culvert and a gal's breath

Picture – Imagine he doesn't really have a goatee, but he stuck a **culvert** on his chin. A gal walked up, and the **gal**'s **breath** was blown on the culvert and it fell off and smashed. She must have some bad breath. As you review make sure you don't confuse him with Mr. Bloomquist who also has a goatee. You will remember that Mr. Bloomquist did not have a moustache along with his goatee like Mr. Galbreath. The review process eliminates confusion.

Face # 77 – Vick Rudolph – Lines under Nose

Sound-Alikes – Vicks salve and Rudolph the red-nosed reindeer

Picture – Imagine **Rudolph** scratched his face and put the lines under his nose. To get some relief he spread **Vicks** salve on the lines.

Face # 78 – Polly Weiskopf – Bun Hairdo - I might not use this feature unless I was sure she wore it all of the time.

Sound-Alikes – Polly the parrot and a wise cough

Picture – Imagine **Polly** the parrot flew up and perched on the bun in her hair. The parrot says, "I'm a real **wise** guy." The lady is allergic to birds and starts to **cough** violently, and her bun unravels.

Review faces 73 through 78 again at this point. During the review process if you happen to forget a name simply go back and look at the name and the face another time to lock the facial picture in more securely. Now review faces 1 through 78.

Face # 79 – Wendy Hines – Thin Eyebrows

Sound-Alikes – Windy and Heinz "57" sauce

Picture – Imagine it was **windy,** and the wind blew her eyebrows totally away. To have some sort of eyebrows she used a pencil and drew eyebrows above her eyes with **Heinz** "57" sauce.

Face # 80 – Darrell Seaver – Partial Thin Sideburns

Sound-Alikes – Dare oil and sea fur

Picture – Imagine he **dare**d a friend to throw **oil** at him, and the friend did. The oil dissolved most of his sideburns. The friend said, "Look, I see a patch of **sea fur.** You can stick it on for sideburns." The fur must have come from a sea otter. Imagine that you see him sticking the sea fur onto his face.

Face # 81 – Sibyl Baker – Ski Nose

Sound-Alikes – Sip oil and a baker

Picture – Imagine a **baker** hung some of his baked goods on her ski nose. There is plenty of room for lots of baked goods. Some of the baking oil begins to drip down, and she **sip**s the **oil** into her mouth.

Face # 82 – Freeman Vedder - Freckles

Sound-Alikes – A free man and wetter (When pronounced with a certain foreign accent wetter becomes Vedder.)

Picture – Imagine he asks friends to pick his freckles off of his face. He says, "Don't worry, they are **free man.**" When they started to pick them off he got excited and started to sweat. His face got **wetter** and wetter (**Vedder**).

Face # 83 – Warren Furst – Fuzzy hair

Sound-Alikes – A war in something and first place in a race or event

Picture – Imagine a **war** took place **in** his hair, and the shooting shot off most of his hair. Soldiers start to run out of his hair and one of them says, "I'm the **first** one out and the **first** to say this war is over."

Face # 84 – Tom Thorne – One Elongated Pupil

Sound-Alikes – A tom-tom and a thorn

Picture – Imagine he was playing a **tom**-tom, and a **thorn** on the tom-tom flew up and stuck in his eye. The thorn caused his pupil to elongate. You might remember that I used a tom-tom for the last name Thomas. It doesn't confuse me. This is a first name and not a last name, and I can always put a map of the US in my picture if I think there will be any confusion.

Review faces 79 through 84 again at this point. During the review process if you happen to forget a name simply go back and look at the name and the face another time to lock the facial picture in more securely. Now review faces 1 through 84.

Face # 85 – Scott Brady – Thick Short Eyebrows
Sound-Alikes – A scout and a braid
Picture – Imagine a Boy **Scout** walked up and began to **braid** his eyebrows to earn a merit badge.

Face # 86 – Mona Robbins – Slanted Eyes
Sound-Alikes – Moan and robins
Picture – Imagine two **robins** are pulling on the edge of each eye like they are pulling on a worm. That is why her eyes are slanted. Of course, it hurts, and she **moan**s loudly.

Face # 87 – Leonard Glass – Long Beard and no Moustache
Sound-Alikes – Lean hard and glass
Picture – Imagine he has grown a long **glass** beard. Someone **lean**s on it very **hard** and the glass beard shatters.

Face # 88 – Kevin Hodges – Curly Hair
Sound-Alikes – Cave in and hedges
Picture – Imagine his curly hair is actually **hedges**. A gardener begins to trim them and the curly hedges **cave in**. An avalanche of hedge hair cascades down his face after the cave in.

Face # 89 – Ben Trammell – Handle Bar Moustache
Sound-Alikes – A wooden bin or to bend something and to trample or a tram and oil
Picture – Imagine you try very hard to **ben**d his handle bar mous-

tache, but it just won't bend. He must use some of Rollie Finger's moustache wax. When you can't bend it by hand you begin to jump up and down on it to **trample** it down.

Face # 90 – Claire Pollard - Birthmark
Sound-Alikes – An eclair and pull hard
Picture – Imagine you threw an **eclair** at her and caused the birthmark. You then **pull** on it very **hard** to try to remove it.

Review faces 85 through 90 again at this point. During the review process if you happen to forget a name simply go back and look at the name and the face another time to lock the facial picture in more securely. Now review faces 1 through 90.

Face # 91 – Rod Michaels – Turned Down Mouth
Sound-Alikes – A steel rod or a fishing rod and my gulls
Picture – Imagine his turned down mouth remind you of the turned down wings of **my gulls**. See yourself swinging a steel **rod** or a fishing **rod** at **my gulls** to shoo them away.

Face # 92 – Reece Parker - Wart
Sound-Alikes – Grease and a parker (one who parks a car)
Picture – Imagine a young man backs a very small car into his wart as he tries to **park** her. **Grease** flies out of the car and covers his wart.

Face # 93 – Ethel Frieberg - Dimples

Sound-Alikes – Ethyl gas and to fry a berg (an iceberg)

Picture – Imagine you pour **ethyl** gas into her dimples. Afterwards you place a frying pan on her dimples, light the **ethyl** gas and begin to **fry** an ice**berg**. It shouldn't take long to fry an iceberg.

Face # 94 – Dixie Utterback – Ponytails

Sound-Alikes – A Dixie cup and udder back

Picture – Imagine her ponytails are the tits hanging down from a cow's udder. See yourself milking the udder into a **Dixie** cup. Afterwards you flip the **udder** to the **back** of her head.

Face # 95 – Joe Ledbetter – High Cheekbones

Sound-Alikes – G. I. Joe and lead better (one who bets)

Picture – Imagine a macho G. I. **Joe** hit him with both of his fists and knocked his cheekbones up very high. Someone comes along later and says, "I'm not much of a **better**, but I'll bet his cheeks don't contain **lead** or they would drop." He is a **lead better**.

Face # 96 – George Moss – Receding Hairline

Sound-Alikes – A gorge and moss

Picture – Imagine his receding hairline reminds you of two **gorge**s. He wants more hair, but it won't grow, so he plants **moss** in the gorges.

Review faces 91 through 96 again at this point. During the review process if you happen to forget a name simply go back and look at the name and the face another time to lock the facial picture in more securely. Now review faces 1 through 96.

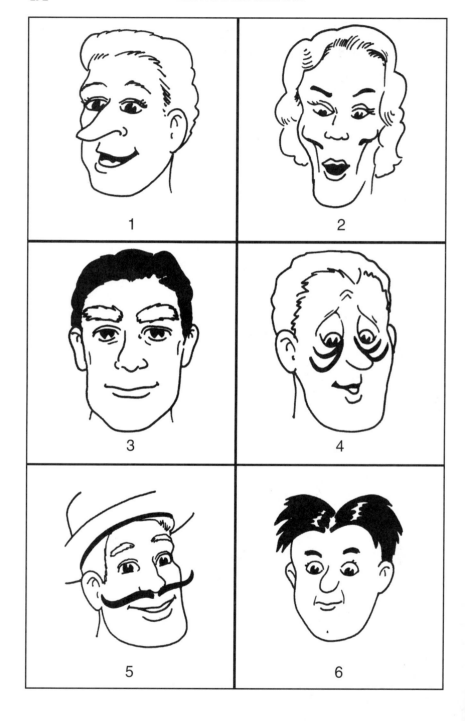

7

8

9

10

11

12

25

26

27

28

29

30

31

32

33

34

35

36

37

38

39

40

41

42

43

44

45

46

47

48

49

50

51

52

53

54

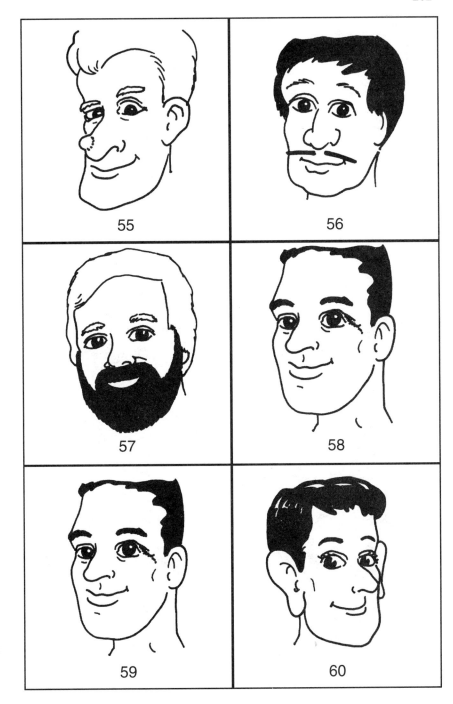

55

56

57

58

59

60

67

68

69

70

71

72

73

74

75

76

77

78

79

80

81

82

83

84

85

86

87

88

89

90

91

92

93

94

95

96

Now that you have completed the **Feature Faces** drill you are ready to begin with actual people. Download my Skill Builder cards from the web site and begin to use them on a regular basis instead of throwing away valuable time. Those who do are those who succeed. Be a doer! The address for the Doctor Memory™ web site and the code for entering the names and faces assistance section are on page 209.

You have learned standards for over 200 names as you worked through the practice faces and feature faces drills. You will learn thousands of standards in the dictionaries of first and last names made available on Doctor Memory's™ web site. The address of the site and the special access code for names and faces are in the back of this book.

You have learned a system that works! What you do with it depends on you. Have **a little bit of discipline** and be an **ODD** person, and you will be successful. Good luck and have good memories.

Doctor Memory™ Web Site

To enter the Doctor Memory™ web site go to:

http://www.doctormemory.com

The special access code for the names
and faces auxiliary material is:

NAF001DM

Other Doctor Memory™ Products

All Dr. Memory™ products use the Lucas Learning System™ where visually reinforced association models make learning fun and easy. Dr. Memory™ teaches Learning That Lasts™. Please visit the web site at   for up-to-date information on the complete product line. Included are descriptions of the complete Learning That Lasts™ product line, as well as actual demonstrations. Excerpts of many of the products are available free of charge also. Doctor Memory™ revolutionary products are available for purchase at doctormemory.com and bookstores. These products include the following:

Adult - Young Adult General Interest

Doctor Memory's™
Picture Perfect Spanish
A Survival Guide to Speaking Spanish

Doctor Memory's™ Learning That Lasts™ methodology is adapted to learn more than 600 "Survival" words required for basic communication of the Spanish language. Careful attention has been paid to insure that the most critical words are taught and that each word is associated with the English equivalent in a way that guarantees accurate pronunciation. In this course, the Spanish language is explored primarily through commonly used words. The addition of basic sentence structure, common phrases and sentences complete the materials; which are designed to prepare the reader to speak the Spanish language more thoroughly than that which is typically covered in a one-year Spanish foreign language course. In addition to teaching over 600 words this book teaches phrases, sentences and basic rules of sentence structure required to speak Spanish.

Doctor Memory's™
Comprehensive Picture Perfect Spanish
Your Reference to the Spanish Language

Doctor Memory's™ Learning That Lasts™ methodology is adapted to aid in the memorization of over 1,600 of the most commonly used Spanish words in this four-volume set. Careful attention has been paid to insure that each word is associated with the English equivalent in a way that guarantees accurate pronunciation. This comprehensive reference teaches words, more detailed grammar, basic sentence structure, conjugation of verbs and more while also exploring common phrases and sentences typical of the Spanish language.

Doctor Memory's™
Learning How to Learn
The Ultimate Learning and Memory Instruction

Doctor Memory's™ unique learning methodology is taught in detail in this comprehensive follow-up to the best selling The Memory Book that was co-authored by Mr. Lucas in 1973. Learning How to Learn teaches the reader how to apply the Learning That Lasts™ methodology to any subject matter. All eight tools of learning developed by Jerry Lucas are taught in detail. Hundreds of applications are discussed and illustrated. Taking almost 30 years to compile, this is the most innovative and comprehensive learning instruction book ever written!

Childrens' Educational Products

Doctor Memory's™
Ready Set Remember
States & Capitals and The Presidents

Doctor Memory's™ unique Learning That Lasts™ methodology is adapted to children's social studies to instruct the memorization of the states, their capitals, and the presidents of the United States. This book with accompanying audio cassettes will guide the learning process and is ideal for either self-directed students or for use in a more traditional classroom environment. An interactive computer based training version is currently under development and will include animation to assist in learning the geographic location of each state as well.

Doctor Memory's™
Grammar Graphics & Picture Perfect
Punctuation - Volume I

Designed for students, teachers, and adults, this first in an eight volume series includes fun and unique pictures that "lock in" the application and usage of the fundamental rules of grammar and punctuation. Doctor Memory's™ revolutionary learning methodology makes even grammar and punctuation fun and easy to learn.

Doctor Memory's™
Ready Set Remember The Times Tables

Doctor Memory's™ unique learning methodology is adapted to assist in the memorization of the times tables from 2x2 to 12x12. This book teaches a simple and fun method of seeing numbers tangibly. Each problem is then pictured in a unique way in order to differentiate it from the others.

For Families that Wish to Study the Bible Together

Doctor Memory's™
Bible Memory Made Easy

Doctor Memory's™ unique Learning That Lasts™ methodology is adapted to help students of any age to better understand and remember Bible facts in this eight volume video tape series. Students learn the Books of the Bible, the Ten Commandments, the Fruit of the Spirit, selected Bible verses, Gifts of the Spirit, and much more. Just by watching and listening you will learn and remember many of the important teachings of the Bible!

Doctor Memory's™
Bible Basics

A fun and easy way for the whole family to learn together! Doctor Memory's™ unique Learning That Lasts™ methodology is adapted to help students of any age to better understand and remember Bible facts. Students learn the Books of the Bible, the Ten Commandments, the Fruit of the Spirit, Gifts of the Spirit, and much more as they discover how fun and easy learning can be with this book and two accompanying audio cassettes.

Doctor Memory's™
View-A-Verse™
Bible Verse Learning Program

Doctor Memory's™ unique Learning That Lasts™ methodology has been adapted to help students of all ages memorize Bible verses simply and easily by seeing the verses tangibly on learning cards that can be reviewed much like everyday flash cards. However, when the verses are pictured and associated with commonly everyday objects, two amazing things will happen. First, the verses are easily learned and memorized. Second, when the commonly used everyday objects are seen in real life, the verses will be automatically remembered bringing the Word of God to mind throughout the day! Learning Bible verses has never been so easy or fun.

Soon to be Released Products for Reading and Writing

Doctor Memory's™
Alphabet Friends™

Doctor Memory's™ unique Learning That Lasts™ methodology is adapted to children's reading and writing in this alphabet and phonetic sound recognition program. Each letter is pictured graphically so as to guarantee the student learns to recognize and write upper and lower case shapes. All possible sounds made by each letter are pictured tangibly, so the student can see and never forget them. This revolutionary product is the first ever published that allows students to actually see all of the sounds tangibly. The student also learns how to read words that include the basic sounds. An interactive computer based training version will be available as well as traditional workbooks with instruction manuals.

Doctor Memory's
See and Know Picture Words™ Reading Program

Doctor Memory's™ unique Learning That Lasts™ methodology is adapted to children's reading in this sight word recognition program. Two hundred twenty words (220) make up 75% of what students will read through the sixth grade and 50% of all words an adult will read throughout their lifetime. All of these "sight" words are pictured graphically to guarantee the student learns the words permanently. Recognition of all significant sounds made within the English language are also taught, including silent letters, letters that change sounds, and the common consonant sound combinations such as "ch" and "th". After completing this course the student will tangibly see and know every sound in the English language while being able to read and pronounce new words. Doctor Memory's™ Alphabet Friends™ is a pre-requisite to this program which will be available in a computer based training version or a more traditional workbook with accompanying instruction manual.

Give the gift of Learning That Lasts™
to your family, friends, and colleagues.

Check with your favorite bookstore or place your order
by logging onto our website.

www.doctormemory.com

....

FOR MAIL ORDERS, PLEASE COMPLETE THIS ORDER FORM:

☐ YES, I want _____ copies of **Names & Faces Made Easy** at $17.95 each,
plus $5.95 shipping and handling for U.S. orders (or $9.70 shipping and handling
for foreign orders). Non-U.S. orders must be accompanied by a postal money
order in U.S. funds. Please allow 3-4 weeks for delivery within the United States
and 6 weeks for delivery elsewhere.

**Call the toll-free phone number noted below
for assitance with completing this order form.**
(please note: we cannot accept cash, personal checks or C.O.D.'s)

Names & faces Made Easy @ $17.95 per book　= $_____
Add appropriate shipping charge (as noted above)　= $_____
Add applicable sales tax*　= $_____
TOTAL PAYMENT　= $_____
***Include sales tax where required.**

Check One:

☐ Money Order or ☐ Cashier's Check (payable to Lucas Educational Systems, Inc.)
☐ Visa　☐ Master Card　☐ Discovery　☐ American Express

Ship to: (please print)

Name_____

Organization_____

Street Address_____

City/State/Zip_____

Phone_____E-Mail_____

Credit Card #_____Exp. Date_____

Signature_____

*For mailing instructions call our
toll free order hot line:*
1-877-479-6463

1-930853-01-7